# Anything school can do YOU can do Better

*The story of a family who learned at home…*
*by Máire Mullarney*

ARLEN
HOUSE

**ARLEN HOUSE, Dublin**
in association with
Marion Boyars, London and New York

© Máire Mullarney, 1983
ISBN 0 905223 38 1


Typesetting by: Redsetter Ltd., Dublin.
Printed by: Irish Elsevier Printers, Shannon
Published by Arlen House, 69 Jones Road,
Dublin 3, Ireland in association with
Marion Boyars, 18 Brewer St., London WIR 4AS
and Marion Boyars Inc., 457 Broom St.,
New York 10012.

# CONTENTS

# Acknowledgements

TO OFFER thanks or acknowledgement to Sean, my husband, would be rather like thanking myself. Naturally, without him there would not have been any children to take part in our unintentional experiment. More important in the context of this book, it was he who found the book by Professor Culverwell on which the whole affair depended, he, too, who made the geometrical insets, the 'long stairs' and much else. If the word 'we' in the early chapters becomes 'I' later on, it is because he was so much engaged in sustaining the whole enterprise that he had to miss much of the fun of 'lessons'.

My first thanks, then, to the half-dozen publishers who said amiable things about the first draft of the book, but sent it back again. But for them, and for Nuala Fennell, who put me in touch with Arlen House, I would not have had the satisfying experience of working with and for a team of Irishwomen who understood me, and whom I understood. Second thanks, then, to my constructive editors, Terry Prone and Janet Martin, and to directors Catherine Rose and Dr Margaret MacCurtain, O.P. The latter had nothing directly to do with this book, and will be surprised to find herself here, but a brilliant lecture of hers on children and mathematics, given maybe fifteen years ago, did a great deal to give me confidence.

Next I should like to thank Hunter Diack, Ivan Illich, Professor J. McVicar Hunt, Dr. Graham Curtis Jennings, and Dr. Burton L. White, who is Director of the Harvard Pre-School Project, for various most helpful communications during recent years.

I should like to acknowledge my debt to the following for their kind permission to quote extracts from the books mentioned: Evans Bros. for *Reading and Reading Failure* by John M. Hughes, (1975); William Collins Sons and Co. Ltd. for *Children's Minds* by Margaret Donaldson, (1978); McGibbon & Kee Ltd. for *The Home and the School* by J. W. B. Douglas, (1964); Methuen & Co. Ltd. for *Love and Hate,* by I. Eibl-Eidesfeldt, (1971); and the Oxford University Press for *The School in Question* by Thorsten Husén, (1979).

*Máire Mullarney,*
*Dublin, 1983.*

# Introduction

IN THE late forties, when our family began, 'early cognitive learning' was not supposed to be possible. It was taken for granted that real learning happened in school, and that school was a good thing; the more of it everyone could get, the better.

Now, in the early eighties, many people, though not all, have come to change their minds radically on both questions. It happens that our experience cuts across both trends. Our children began to learn early, and they learnt at home, not at school, until the age of eight or nine. Now that the youngest of our eleven children has just finished school, it seems that the learning they did in those few years at home has been much more relevant to their later careers than anything they did in primary school. As for post-primary school, some gained some benefit, when they were lucky enough to meet a good teacher with a small class; two at least were harmed; on the whole, the experience was irrelevant.

The first part of this book tells about the early learning; how it was prompted, and a general survey of how we all went about it. Anyone who wants to make use of our experience will find more detail in a chapter called *Resources*, towards the end.

The next section gives a short account of each of the children, just to tie up the beginnings with their life after school. It might be easier to keep track of the people moving through the first story if you turn to these chapters if confused.

Then comes *The Reading Question* with a chapter to itself. This is a subject which, in the English speaking world, generates vast amounts of argument. There are those who think reading is too delicate a matter for parents to meddle in and there are others who think that parents should be enlisted to help the school. There are those who think it should be taught in kindergarten, and others who vehemently disagree. I have just come across this judgement, made in 1970 by Dr Hans Furth, a psychologist at the Catholic University of America, Washington, DC.

Mark well these twin conditions: learn reading and forget your intellect. The average five to nine year old, from any environment, is unlikely, when busy with reading and writing, to engage his intellectual powers to any degree.

Even to copy that sentence makes my blood pressure rise. And on top of the disagreement about when reading should be taught, and by whom, there are entrenched views about the best methods. We used four different methods; though each did well enough one of them seemed decidedly more satisfactory than the others; it is appropriate only to the home. In the first draft of this book I found that while I was trying to describe our experience I was also getting caught up in arguments on all fronts at once. This time round I have tried to give a straight account of the different methods in the first part of the book and keep all the arguments and references to research which I discovered later on safely shut up in a chapter of their own.

Children learning at home need one or two parents at home as well. The changes in attitudes towards school are small compared with the changed view of women's role. It should be evident from the first part of the book that I found staying at home with interested children much more fun than either of the 'jobs' that I had had beforehand. This is a view that many women will find most unwelcome. Here I will say no more than that everything would have been quite different if I had just been minding the family, keeping them clean and fed; it was the learning together that gave zest to the days, even though it took only a little time. But this solution has so many implications that it also needs a chapter of its own — *Reflections*.

I have just written, in the opening paragraph, that attitudes both to school and to early learning have changed radically since the forties and fifties. There is no reason why readers should have to take this on faith. In the matter of early learning, I can produce most telling evidence from Professor J. McVicar Hunt of the University of Illinois. He was speaking to assembled psychologists when he said, in 1963:

> Even as late as 15 years ago, a symposium on the stimulation of early cognitive learning would have been taken as a sign that the participants and members of the audience were too softheaded to be taken seriously.

Now, if you go back fifteen years from 1963 you find yourself in 1948 — the very year in which we had begun to busy ourselves with showing an eight month-old baby how to fit squares and triangles into matching spaces.

There hardly seems to be any need to prove that 'early cognitive development' is now a focus of interest. I suspect that Professor Hunt's book, *Intelligence and Experience*, published in 1961, may have set the ball rolling. By the 1970s millions of dollars were being invested in America in 'Head Start'. I have read in the last few months of the most astonishing, even alarming, campaigns for early stimulation being launched in Venezuela, in Bulgaria, in Japan and China. The Venezuelan one, at least, is based directly on the findings of the Harvard Pre-School Project, reported on by Dr Burton L. White in 1972, funded by Head Start.

I have beside me *Child Alive* (Lewin) published in London in 1975, a collection of articles published in *New Scientist* during the previous year. Two significant sentences from preface and blurb:

> All the researchers agree on one thing, however: that the newborn human infant has been grossly underestimated, and that we are now beginning to learn just how wrong the old ideas were! . . . Interestingly, some of these results back up the intuitive beliefs of parents, who turn out to have been responding to their own children far better than the older findings of psychology would have led them to.

That school was assumed to be a good thing can be seen from the laws that compelled attendance at age five in Britain, six in the USA, seven in Finland, and efforts to make similar laws realistic in developing countries. At the same time there seems to have been a more easygoing attitude to those who avoided attendance. The great New England artist Andrew Wyeth mentions in a published conversation that as a child he was frail and never went to formal schools; when he goes on to tell how his father taught him to paint he describes, it seems to me, the very ideal of education. (*The Two Worlds of Andrew Wyeth*, Boston 1978). Nowadays the time spent on schoolgoing gets longer and longer and escape seems more difficult. John Holt's newsletter, *Growing Without Schooling*, demonstrates that many parents in the USA who want to teach their children at home have to fight for the privilege.

It is not surprising that while emphasis on the importance of school increases reaction against it should be more evident. It was only in 1971 that Ivan Illich wrote *Deschooling Society* but three or four years later there had been enough debate on the topic to give material for a collection of papers published by the Cambridge University Press under the simple title, *Deschooling* (see bibliography under Lister). Even more recently, in 1979, *The School in Question* shows that there is a more impressive convert to the counter-school movement. The author, Thorsten Husén, is Professor of Education in the University of Stockholm, founder of the Swedish comprehensive school system and director of world-wide research. As recently as 1970 he saw the need for change but still believed it would come *through* schools; in this book he indicates that bureaucracy, inertia and the conflicting demands made on teachers combine to make it impossible for the school system to cure itself.

If those inside cannot repair the system it is up to those outside to move. *Anything School Can Do, You Can Do Better* is my contribution. After some eighteen quiet years of child-watching I had come to realise that school was a time-wasting and inefficient attempt to enable one generation to share knowledge with the next. When the elders felt the need to subdue the young by beating and humiliating them, that went beyond mere

9

inefficiency. It had not dawned on me that sharing knowledge was only a minor purpose of the system. I began to write an occasional letter to *The Irish Times*, then articles sent here and there. When I ventured to send one to *The Irish Times* it was published within a few days and I was asked for more. Marvellous. I went on to write about other things but with so many children growing up I could hardly forget the question of schooling. I have found that it is impossible to give a balanced account of my views and my experience in short articles, hence this book — which could so easily be twice as long.

Who do I hope will read it? It must go without saying that I would like to provide support for parents who are disillusioned with the school systems that exist. It would be better still to find readers among young people who see their own schooldays not far behind, their role as parents not far ahead, and who would like to make some changes. Is it startling to recognise that in our society schooling of one kind or another is now likely to be a dominant preoccupation from the age of four or five until the age of forty-five or fifty when one can hope to see one's youngest child over most of the hurdles?

Even now it is extremely encouraging to find that mothers who campaign for natural childbirth and breastfeeding seem to move on spontaneously into taking a more active responsibility for their children's learning. Fathers and children as well come to meetings of La Leche League; when I was asked to speak to them on this topic I found them the most casual, agreeable audience I had ever met.

There is an affinity also between environmentalists, those interested in self-reliance and healthy living, and de-schoolers. I should not be surprised if quite a few readers turn out to be parents who did much the same thing themselves but never said anything about it. Still, taking everything into account, I do not believe there is anyone to whom this book could be more valuable than to a Minister of Education who is running short of funds, as they all are now.

# Chapter 1
# THE BEGINNING

IT WOULD be difficult for beginner parents to be more ignorant of children and children's development than we were. Sean was an only child. I was not much better; for five years I had had a little brother, but he was a Down's Syndrome baby, loving and lovable, but misleading as an example of how ordinary children learn.

Not only were we short of brothers and sisters, and consequently of nephews and nieces, we had no neighbouring children to observe either. Worse still, I had qualified as a State Registered Nurse at a time when junior nurses were trained to keep children quiet and neat in their little beds and to look on parents as a disturbing influence.

We began our life as a family in a small cottage some twelve miles to the south of Dublin city. It was two steep miles from public transport. Our only neighbours, just above us on the hillside, were the two bachelor brothers from whom we had bought our house. This isolation enabled us to live, unawares, twenty-five years ahead of our time, to experiment with early education without having any intention of experimenting.

If we had been able to settle for a family of two or three I daresay we would have forgotten all about these activities; I certainly would not have thought of writing about them. But instead of two or three we ended up, unintentionally, with a family of eleven, five girls and six boys. Instead of having a passing glimpse of what is now called 'early cognitive development' I was wrapped up in it for twenty years, and found towards the end that it was beginning to become a respectable subject for research. This, then, is not a scientific report; it is the story of ordinary parents who had unusually prolonged and varied opportunities for own-child-watching. If we had been qualified to make scientific reports we would not have been ordinary parents, would we?

Since we had so little notion of what anyone else was doing it did not occur to us for a long time that our habits were at all unusual. Indeed, I suspect that formal learning at home is both more usual and more useful than the authorities like to admit. Once we came to recognise how heavily people relied on school, we began to stack away a few workbooks, so that if some powerful inspector should call we would be able to show that the children were mastering the basic skills. Many, many drawings and paintings were preserved also, and we began to put names and dates on these once we had learnt how surprisingly easy it is to get mixed up.

When Barbara, the eldest, was twelve, she organised a Birthday Book for Seán's birthday, with contributions of some kind from each of her brothers and sisters, right down to the current baby. This she brought out again each year and even when she had left home we carried on. This volume helps to keep memories in sequence. So do some of the articles that I began to write for newspapers and magazines towards the end of the 'experiment', when the youngest baby was about two.

The small house where we began to learn from our children was neither old enough to be picturesque nor new enough to have piped water or electricity. It consisted of four small square rooms in a block, with another little room tacked on the south end. This last sheltered a corner we called the patio, which was as much used as any room indoors. The house could be found at the end of a narrow lane, in a half-acre garden, just on the border between gorse and bracken and some struggling fields. In our time there were few trees; our bachelor neighbours saw trees simply as firewood standing up.

It was the boast of the brothers that we lived in 'a great place for drying turf'. (Turf, or peat, is very wet when it is cut out of bogland and it has to be dried in the air before being used as fuel). True enough, the wind used to whirl through our house from back to front so that you could almost dry turf indoors. Boiling, including nappies (diapers) was done on a primus stove; I baked in a pot-oven on the turf fire. Along with the turf we used dried branches of gorse from the hillside.

Lighting was by candle and oil lamp. Water came straight from heaven into barrels placed around the house. For drinking we preferred water from the spring some fifty yards away. The road was so rough that it was difficult to have anything delivered; turf was left half-way up the hill and collected by one of the brothers with a horse and cart. Anything else, including timber and paint for renovations, came up in our own arms.

Life was not simple, but it *was* delightful. If I had to lug buckets of water from the spring, I carried them past blackberry hedges, through fields thick with corn-marigolds and wild pansies. Looking up from the flowers I would see Killiney Head with Dalkey Island sailing away from it, Howth lying in the background on the far side of Dublin Bay. In the mornings the sun used to come straight out of the sea into our bedroom window, and by mid-morning it was warming the sheltered patio and the small, bookshelf-lined sitting-room.

We learned to grow our own vegetables on the half acre. Never before or since those days have I had more fresh peas than I could manage to eat. We found that we loved nettle soup and fairy-ring-mushroom omelettes. The soil produced wonderful strawberries, too.

True, one winter storm washed away the road completely; strange cars were at intervals bogged down in the mud at the bottom of our lane and I would have to go and help to dig them out. Whenever there was snow it stayed with us so that I had to bathe the children's feet in warm water every few hours in order to ward off chilblains. Sean bought Canadian lumberjack boots to get down to the train, and his colleagues at the office — he is an accountant — naturally found them diverting.

That such isolation was possible, just twelve miles from Dublin, seems all the more unlikely today when the rugged hillside lanes have been properly tarmacadamed, the bare mountainside covered in Forestry Commission trees, there are smart houses everywhere and the wilderness has been driven back. But at that time it was a lonely cottage with a minute, and therefore suitable, mortgage. It took four years for electricity to reach us, six for the telephone to be connected. We never bought a car. Yet we seemed to manage without going near a shop for weeks on end.

The first thing people ask when they discover that the children learned at home is, 'How did you find time?' In fact, my share of the activity did not take any extra time. I moved the baby around with me, either on one arm or in the Moses basket. Gardening, sewing, cooking and reading fit in with paying some attention to a baby. We would lie on a rug together, indoors or out; baby on tummy, a mirror to reach for; on her back, kicking at a sheet of coloured paper held by parent; or parent on back, arms straight up, holding flying baby.

It was when each child was able to get around independently, crawling and walking, that time spent in shared activity showed itself to be an investment. Babies who have had a solid chunk of full parental attention feel confident enough to potter around and explore for the rest of the day, making contact from time to time. By the time the early members of our family were reaching the age of four or five, my involvement was greater, especially as there were more little people around, but the older ones were doing most of their planned learning on their own while I was saved the time-consuming task of getting self, child and baby (or babies) dressed up for escort duty to and from school or nursery school.

There were other gains. Instead of the gap, which begins when the school-going child is five and unable to fully answer the question 'What did you do in school today?' and which widens into a gulf between home and school later on, there were shared areas of interest and knowledge. Conformity was kept to a minimum. It bothers me to hear a five-year-old wanting to wear the same kind of T-shirt everybody else is wearing.

Eliminated, too, was the inevitable postponement of the learning of skills which happens in nursery and primary schools, where it is necessary, before skills can be learned, for the children simply to come to terms with the relatively large numbers involved and to develop a 'substitute parent' image of the teacher. In schools for young children much time also goes in developing 'group consciousness'. But how much group consciousness do we need? In later life, unless we join the army or a large religious community, we hardly ever need to think of ourselves as one of a group of thirty. It is, on the other hand, extremely valuable to be able to do things by yourself, even to be comfortable alone, without company. It is possible that too much group consciousness too soon may result in adults who cannot be alone.

Each baby lived out its first fifteen months in a 'Moses basket', large enough to lie down in, light enough for carrying. In good weather it was parked where there were people or plants to be looked at and in bad weather basket and baby were propped into a large packing-case, arranged with its back to the wind.

The basket served the purpose of a playpen as well as that of a pram or cot. A baby lying down could kick crumpled sheets of brown paper tucked into the end and make a satisfying noise. Propped up, he or she could lounge or sit, join in conversation, play with items on a cord stretched across the top, or chew an apple. There was also the possibility of falling asleep in comfort at any moment. Of course, they also wanted to be picked up, and I became quite accomplished, like so many before me, at sweeping or stirring or mixing cakes with one hand while holding baby on my hip with the other arm.

All of these habits arose naturally. The idea of developing them into a home-education system came later.

# Chapter 2
# ENTER MONTESSORI

EVER SINCE he was a small boy Sean had been haunting the Dublin bookstalls. Indeed, it was because he always had a book under his arm when he used to come as an out-patient to the hospital department where I was working that I first took note of him. When our eldest daughter was a few months old he bought for fourpence a book that was going to make quite a difference to the future family.

This book was *The Montessori Method*, by Professor E. P. Culverwell, published in 1912. The author was Professor of Education in Trinity College, Dublin, therefore an informed as well as an objective observer. He visited the 'Children's Houses' in Rome and saw how the method worked in its early stages, before any practices had become rigid; he could distinguish the essentials in the new approach and he even made some very good guesses about the kind of adult it might produce. For us, to whom the whole idea was quite new, this book, written in decent English, was much more attractive than Dr Montessori's own books, translated from the Italian, would have been.

However, anyone who is prompted to take an interest in Montessori's discoveries should certainly go back to the source and read her own story, told by herself. (See bibliography). Maria Montessori, born in 1870, was the first woman to qualify as a doctor of medicine in Italy. It is interesting that she had first planned to be an engineer! She won the gold medal for her year. The first job found for her was the care of retarded children. She noticed that the children, for whom no occupation was provided, used to play with breadcrumbs rolled into balls. She proceeded to read everything written about such children and to invent materials which would help them to learn. By the age of twenty-eight she was Director of a state school.

When the retarded children from her school were entered for

State examinations they succeeded as well as normal children. For Montessori, this was only the beginning.

> 'I was searching', she wrote, 'for the reasons which could keep happy healthy children of the common schools on so low a plane that they could be equalled in tests of intelligence by my unfortunate pupils.'

The next step came with the opportunity to try her methods with normal children. The owners of some blocks of flats offered Montessori rooms in which her assistants could look after the young children of working mothers. She called each set of rooms a Children's House — *Casa dei Bambini*. The first was opened in 1907; by 1912 she had been invited to lecture in the United States of America, was much valued by Thomas Edison, by Alexander Graham Bell, by the President of the time, Woodrow Wilson. In 1917 Freud, who had been asked to sign some appeal along with her, wrote, '. . . the opposition which my name could arouse in public opinion must be overpowered by the brilliance which emanates from yours.' In short, it was widely recognised that she had made sigrnificant discoveries about children's development.

But remember that when we found Professor Culverwell's book we knew nothing about all that had happened after its publication. We knew nothing either about later reactions. We simply liked the look of what we read. Montessori said that human beings have an appetite for learning, that they find the right sort of work satisfying; that there seem to be 'sensitive periods' when one kind of work or learning is more attractive and useful than it would be earlier or later.

Like any other people who have a small baby available, we could see that this was true; that it was quite hard work for Barbara to teach herself to crawl and to stand up, but that she could not be contented until she was able to do these things and then she would look for something else to learn.

As we understood it, our job was to have other 'work' waiting. We should try to plan for whatever she might be ready to do next, show her how it should be done, then let her do it or not; if we offered something she was ready for, she would want to do it. If things went wrong, we should think twice before jumping in with a correction; it might be better to offer something else and put away the difficult

17

material until she would be able to do it more easily. And whenever she was concentrating on her 'work', whether it was something we had provided or something she had found for herself, we should respect her attention and avoid interruption unless it was essential.

Now, the children Montessori was talking about were all aged between three and six. We might easily have been impressed by the book and simply decided to look for a Montessori school when the time came. But we did not know whether such schools existed or not, and at least we knew what would be needed just to get to an ordinary school; two miles walk up or down the hill and bus journey the rest of the way. We could not imagine a four or five year-old making that trip every day. At the same time we did not want Barbara to be deprived of anything by what seemed an unavoidably late start. We felt that perhaps we should offer what help we could beforehand.

We began, then, with a baby who had begun to crawl (at about five months) but who still spent a fair amount of time sitting in her basket. Montessori spoke of 'the education of the senses'; sight, touch, sound, smell, awareness of weight. We had been giving the baby things to play with anyway. Now we tried to make sure there was variety in weight and texture; wood, leather, fur, a silver spoon, a brass bell, smooth stones. Rough stones she could find for herself when on a crawling expedition.

She would wave a wooden spoon with a ribbon tied to the handle. If we gave her two cups from a set of plastic nesting cups (see *Resources*), one in each hand, there was a good chance the smaller cup would find its way into the larger. My mother used to make particularly fine stuffed toys (sometimes commissioned as window dressing by good stores). Even better, at this stage, were the felt balls. They were made in six sections and stitched on the outside, stuffed with kapok, then firmed up by being dipped in boiling water. These were ideal toys at the crawling stage. They could roll, but not too far. They were easy to grip, and were made in attractive colour combinations. (A much older Barbara made larger balls of papier mâché with bright designs, which turned out to be remarkably good toys for younger children. They were durable and incapable of doing damage).

All through the summer, that first year and every other year, there was a shallow dish of water in the patio, or out in the front to warm in the morning sun. At six months a child could sit up long enough to dabble the hands. Older babies could pour and spill, fill mugs and measure quantities. In really good weather, of course, they preferred just to sit down in it.

No doubt the grass Barbara crawled on, the mud she sometimes met instead, the woven willow of the basket, the wooden floor boards, the hairy hearth rug were sensory experiences, too. In addition, she had been given a soft, useless nylon baby brush, and developed quite a fondness for its smooth back and soft flexible bristles.

It was not until she was on her feet that we could show her how to stroke furry pansies or crisp daffodils, to sniff them for scent and to find ways of paying attention to these bright objects without pulling their heads off. Any time there was a cat around, the toddler was shown how to stroke the fur in the right direction, just as earlier she had been encouraged to stroke a fur hand-muff.

Nobody was conscious then of the use of mobiles for giving babies extra stimulus. We simply made sure that any basketed baby always had something to look at. Often it was flowers or a waving branch.

We had a gramophone and Seán was brushing up his skill on the piano, so there was some music around for Barbara. Singing I could not provide. It was unfortunate, too, that I was not aware that she needed to hear plenty of chat if she was to start talking herself. Of course I echoed her own burbles and exclamations as every mother does, but I do not think I talked much about what I was doing around the place, so it was not surprising that she was two before she had much to say.

We did play a game based on Montessori's 'Three Steps'. The idea is to give a child a clear idea of what is meant by a particular word. In the ordinary way they have to puzzle it out from conversation. It also helps the adult to know whether the child has understood or not.

If Barbara was, say, turning a spoon around and investigating it, I would wait until the first interest had died down, rather than interrupting, and then would produce a fork.

'Spoon', I would announce, holding it up, and follow it with the other, saying 'Fork'.

The second step was to lay them in front of her, hold out a hand and say, 'Give me spoon?'.

If at that point she gave me the fork or played at hiding, I backtracked and tidied up. If she was interested and gave me the spoon, I would then say, 'Give me fork?' If that was handed over, enthusiastic thanks were forthcoming.

The third of the Montessori Three Steps comes only when the learner has begun to talk. It consists of saying 'What's that?' about each in turn. At a particular point, too, I added the word 'please'. Earlier on I felt it would give the baby the idea that she was eating with an object called a spoonplease.

This formality is a slight elaboration on what parents do instinctively. It has the advantage of comparing two associated objects which makes learning easier, and asking only about things the baby has had a chance to learn, which makes success more likely. The habit is useful at later stages, as I found out.

As Barbara became a little older, and Alasdar came along, we turned our attention to what Montessori called 'didactic material' and what we called 'lesson things'. We made some of them, among them geometric insets, button-frames, sandpaper letters. In the early days we substituted nesting cups, pyramid rings and Chinese boxes for the Montessori Cylinder sets we read about. (See *Resources*).

There were bits of sandpaper and fabric for feeling, metal jars from the chemist to hold hot and cold water, pill boxes for holding rattling objects. Paper from the office, where duplicating machines seemed to make thirty surplus copies of everything, was essential both for lessons and for drawing.

I think it was while lying on the floor or on the rug in the patio watching Barbara intently building, using pyramid rings, that I learned most about early learning. My share at first was to assemble the rings on their peg, one on top of the other, slowly, so that she could see just what was supposed to happen. Then I would take one or two rings off and see if she would try to put them on. Later on I could bring out the complete pyramid, let her take the rings off and try to replace them. She would find that if she did not do it in the right order she would be left with something over at the end, or she might hide a small ring under a larger one. There was no need for me to interrupt with applause when she put a ring in place. Still, when she was able to recognise that she must have covered up the missing ring, and promptly dismantled the pyramid to find it, we would congratulate each other like anything. I could make myself useful by pushing back a ring that might have moved out of her field of vision.

With Barbara and with the others following, months might go by between the first attempt and the time when the task became too easy to be interesting. Still, it does no good to give these purposeful games to a baby too young to see the purpose. I have seen a baby of six months who had been given a similar pyramid, but with rings made of bouncy soft plastic. He threw them around with delight, but had no notion of setting them in order. Nor could he have been expected to. If the material has been offered at the right time, and if the baby chooses it in preference to something else, it will be obvious that she manages a bit better every week. The watchful grown-up will soon see that she can be trusted to teach herself. The main thing to remember is that 'lesson things' cannot be left lying around half done; as soon as concentration seems to be fading, the grown up should construct whatever has to be constructed, or fit in whatever has to be fitted, and put them back on their shelf.

The Geometrical Insets (see *Resources*) turned out to be the backbone of our system. We made our own out of plywood, which we painted, and they lasted well. They combine practice in choice and in discrimination and they are self correcting. When talking about them you are bound to use words like inside, outside, angle, curve, straight, as well as triangle, rectangle, and so on. In their second stage they give particularly good practice in hand-and-eye co-ordination; it seems, too, that they help to clarify the concept of area.

Montessori did not offer her insets until her children were three. We found that babies of eight months, once able to sit without support, were quite ready to make a start. We would pick two shapes that could not fit into each other's spaces; a triangle too large to be enclosed in the circle, a circle that would not fit into the triangle. These would be put down in front of the baby when he or she was obviously in the mood for experiment. First we would lift out the circle, using its little knob, feel slowly all around it with the fingers of the other hand, say 'Circle'. Then we would put it back very slowly, making sure baby was watching, and do the same with the triangle. Then we would take one or other inset out and leave it down, to see if the baby would try to fit it back. That would, usually, be enough for one day, and might take less than ten minutes.

If you associate the idea of 'learning' with a nine-month-old baby trying to fit a triangle into its place, you simply cannot think of punishment in the same context. It would have been very wrong as well as absurd to be angry with the baby who threw around the bouncy rings. Montessori had words of biblical force to reprove adults who import anger and punishment into innocent situations. When you move out into the world and find 'learning' and punishment brought into everyday relationship it appears disgusting.

On the other hand, it is very easy to imagine oneself being tempted to anger if faced with the job of controlling forty active four-year-olds. For this reason I am puzzled when I hear a mother say, 'Teach them at home? I would never have the patience!' What do they think happens in school? Is the teacher, just another human being, expected to be eternally patient with their child, and with thirty-nine others as well, or does it not matter who is angry with the child, provided mother is not made uncomfortable?

To come back to the baby who had been shown the triangle and the circle. Next time we would go through the same procedure, giving the student a chance to fit both insets back or take them out and feel them. We might play the game several times, always using the words *circle* and *triangle*, before asking for them by name. When two insets were familiar, we would change one, offer circle and square instead of circle and triangle. And so on. It is just a question of being guided by the amount of interest the baby shows.

I remember Oliver, the youngest of the family, finding the whole set on a low window sill and putting each item in place correctly when he was fifteen months old. He would not have known all the names, but the matching of shapes was easy. Since then I have seen children of two and a half or three seemingly baffled by plastic puzzles based on the same shapes. There seem to me to be advantages in the early introduction to just two shapes at a time.

Once we had insets, a pyramid and a set of plastic nesting cups we had enough structured material to offer the first babies, so they had the possibility of choice. And, of course, they always had the choice of crawling or running away. But it was easy to add a few more. Buttons and other fastenings hold everyday life together. They played a significant part in Montessori's War of Independence, whose slogan was 'never do anything for a child that he can do for himself'. She was dealing with children who were buttoned and suspendered up to their necks, so she devised a multitude of frames with fabric attached on which the children could learn to fasten and open buttons, laces, hook-and-eyes. We made just one for buttons, one for snapfasteners.

For the education of the senses, we collected small objects to be put into a bag and identified by being felt. There was a smooth piece of wood with strips of rough and smooth sandpaper stuck on, to be felt with the fingertips. In a box I assembled squares of velvet, corduroy, stiff linen, tweed, tapestry, silk and cotton. There were two of each, for matching. The aim was to progress from matching the bits with eyes open to matching them just by feel with the eyes closed.

In matching sounds, I used a xylophone to begin with. I would strike a note and expect the child to strike the same one. Next step was to have it done with closed eyes. At one time, we had a pair of xylophones, which made the game better. Rattley boxes (small boxes with lentils, beads or beans inside) were another way of matching sounds. Very soon, each child learned the rudiments of melody, and promptly lost me. Barbara even taught herself to play the piano, using one of those keyboard charts, when she was nearly seven.

Another game of listening, which was always in demand, was the Silence Game. For this, you need more than two, so it had to wait until the family had grown sufficiently. The children used to arrange themselves in a semi-circle sitting on chairs or stools, feet on the ground, as far from the door as possible. First, they would make themselves comfortable, so coughs and wriggles might be avoided. Then I would suggest that we breathe very quietly, not making a sound, so that we could listen to whatever sounds there were — rain, birds, a mouse or a plane. When they had had as much silence as the youngest could take, I would tiptoe to the door, open it very slowly, then whisper one child's name from outside. The named child had to try to get out without making a sound, then wait equally quietly until the next was called.

Another game led to counting. Right from the beginning, as soon as Barbara could stand up with her hands held, I found myself giving her little jumps. Soon we were counting the jumps up to ten. Years went by and new toddlers were clamouring for jumps, as were the others, up to nine or ten. This game must have helped the younger ones to internalise the meaning of number. It certainly helped them to get splendid bounce, going well up over my head to just miss the kitchen ceiling. (It was only when I spent a couple of weeks teaching a nursery school that I discovered how many children had no bounce at all). Queues of children looking for ten jumps each and then going back to queue for ten more must have done my waistline nothing but good.

Perhaps when these activities are described one after the other in the space of a few pages the impression is given of planned, purposeful days, of a high-pressure system. I can only assure any anxious reader that it wasn't like that at all. During the early years each day touched twice the real time of the world outside; once, when we saw Seán off to his morning train, waited until he reached the bend in the road where he could look back and see us waving; the second, when he would emerge from the evening train, visible far below, and it was time for us to put dinner together and collect the evidence, if any, of the day's work.

No radio, no television, no appointments, no shopping. Very few toys; Barbara's Teddy was more like one of the family than a toy, Alasdar had a small rocking-horse. Sean made a town for them, added a beautiful Noah's Ark with animals and Mr and Mrs Noah. We collected good hardwood blocks. Naturally, they were equally contented to play with these or to complete insets while I was getting on with the washing.

# Chapter 3

# PAINTING, DRAWING, AND MAMA HAS A REST

ONLY I knew which were proper 'lesson things' and which were not. The need for a dividing line in my own head arose because of the importance of ensuring that if there is a right way of using something, then a baby who does not know that way cannot be let play with it. It is no hardship if there are plenty of other things to do. If I found one of the children anxious to get at a button frame when she was only nine months old, I would initially try to distract her. If that failed, we would push a button through a button-hole very slowly together, and I would hang on until she seemed satisfied. I would never leave it with her in the basket, as I might leave a rolling-pin or a candlestick.

We never looked on materials for painting and drawing as 'lesson things', even though they needed some control in the handling. We were never short of paper, thanks to Sean's office. The children could have charcoal, crayons or coloured pencils at any time. Paint I had to mix, so it was not so freely available.

I had heard somewhere that Japanese children are given paint brushes at an early age, with happy results. By the age of six, everyone can paint a chrysanthemum free-hand in a few minutes. With this in mind, when Barbara was about a year old, I gave her some powder paint in a saucer, mixed with water to make a thick cream, and a long-handled paint brush. An enamel table top turned on its side made a good surface to spread colour on, and made it easier to show her how to use the brush. Putting paint on an upright surface does not lend itself to leaning heavily on the brush. Once she had learned that lesson, she could paint on the flat if she wanted to, or on the tiled wall.

This worked so well that no baby went past a year without meeting a paint brush. The Birthday Book has a contribution from seven-month-old Eoin, the second-last of the children. I suspect the intervention of Tinu, who was then aged twelve; on the opposite page she has a drawing of the same Eoin, crawling away.

Before giving Barbara the paint brush, I had given her a bit of charcoal. It seemed obvious to me that a baby who could hold a spoon could hold something that would make a mark on paper. What I did not suspect was that she was rather smart to have been holding that spoon and feeding herself with it, and this independence was all her own work. When I was feeding her she constantly reached for the spoon, and tried to put it in her mouth. At eight or nine months she would hit her eye or her nose, she would hold the spoon upside down, but she got food, or some of it, into her mouth. I would find myself without a spoon, get another and start to use that. Next thing, Barbara would have a spoon in each hand. I soon learned to provide myself with three spoons to start with. By the time she was eleven months old she could be put in front of a plate of mashed potato and vegetable, or banana, or anything else of similar consistency, and spoon the lot up quite tidily. I learned from Barbara the benefit of the Montessori advice not to do anything for a child which she can do for herself. As a result, all of the children were feeding themselves by eleven months.

They could wash their hands quite early too. Then came help with other jobs like sweeping. Washing up, dusting, floor polishing and gardening Montessori called 'exercises of practical life'. She emphasised the need for tools children could really use, and the concomitanty need to show them how to use the tool correctly.

I did my best to follow the Montessori advice to have a place for everything and everything in its place. Children find that some jobs have built-in tidiness. Plates and saucers drain in a plate-rack, but knives and forks have to be dried and put into the proper sections of the knife-box. Polished shoes stay in pairs.

Sweeping dust into a dustpan with a handbrush seems to give a feeling of achievement to people of fifteen to eighteen months. Indeed, in our second house, where we had stairs, I relied for years on infant labour to keep them brushed. In the matter of polishing floors, fairly stable toddlers can slide around with bits of blanket on their feet and be more of a help than a hindrance.

From two upwards they were able to hold a shrub being planted out, and take a special pride in it afterwards. A little later they were able to put peas or beans in a drill. (They did not, after all, have very far to stoop). By the time the peas were ripe for picking, the planter was often able to count how many were in the pods.

While I did not always live up to Montessori's high standards of order in everyday life, I could recognise that it might be very important to a person of two or three, so I tried to make sure that their clothes, shoes, dishes and above all 'lesson things' were kept in the same places, stacked in the same ways. Storage space was always a problem. Empty shelves are as important as a Moses basket.

There was no rigidity, no decision on each morning that we would 'do' a particular set of tasks, structure our learning day in a given way. Instead, some routine tasks proved their value, and became a common factor of almost every day. Two of these were writing patterns and filling insets.

Insets came first. Popping the different shapes (page 120) into place was very easy. The next step was to put the outer piece on paper and run a pencil all around inside like a stencil, to produce the same shape on the paper, and then to fill this outline in with parallel lines. Most of the children were doing this by two-and-a-half or three. They had been using a pencil for a long time, so they had no difficulty. Routine can be restful, and they could see for themselves when they had done better than before. I felt that it had a settling effect, so I often started the morning by asking, 'Which inset are you doing today? Rectangle or ellipse?'

It sounds like blackmail, but in fact they were perfectly well able to opt instead for building a tower or to head for the garden. But as a rule they 'did' an inset most days, and sometimes did as many as a dozen.

In the beginning it was necessary for me to hold the outside of the inset firmly on the piece of paper, while the coloured pencil wobbled its way around the edge. There was satisfaction when the wood was lifted and a neat shape, just the same, was left on the page. Then I might draw a few lines myself, just to demonstrate. I would hand back the pencil, making encouraging noises.

'Try to start *right* on the line . . .'

'A *little* further . . .'

'Could you put a line between those two'? They're very far away from each other . . .'

'That's *very* good. Just make it come all the way to the edge.'

27

At first, of course, the lines were curved and wild, but a straight line from edge to edge had a great attraction, and the finished insets became more and more perfect.

To anyone who objects that this is an unsuitable occupation for children, I reply that no one turns a hair at the practice of giving children boxes of crayons and books full of vulgarly conceived, ill-drawn, crudely printed pictures to be filled with colour. If a sensible adult can see that an accurately filled ellipse is more pleasing than a purple scribbled dog-in-the-manger, why suppose that a child cannot see as much? The children, too, had as much free-hand drawing as they wanted.

When Barbara was nearly three we came across some favourable mention of Marion Richardson's *Writing and Writing Patterns* (see bibliography). We ordered them and were sent a set of six slim books along with an inspiring *Teacher's Book*. We found that their designer put much emphasis on painting and tracing so that, although the books were intended for children of five or six and upward, the general approach was attractive to our three-year-old. Later on I found these books in use in two or three different schools; in every case it was obvious from the way in which they were used that the teacher had not read the manual addressed to her. We found that the children who were already acquiring good control of their pencil through work with geometrical insets found this way of progressing towards writing was satisfying. These two exercises were the routine part of everyday learning for many years, and produced half-a-dozen adults with good or excellent handwriting.

With so much going on in the daytime, and with nights that were usually disturbed, I badly needed a break in the middle of the day. I felt that it was as important for the children that I should be relaxed as it was for myself. When Barbara was small I could use the time of her afternoon rest to lie down. When there were two or three slightly older children, I used to put them to rest in their own room, close the door and hope for the best. Later again, I could leave them free, but lock them out of my own room while I had my siesta. By that time I was able to explain to them that it was in their own interest to keep Mama in good humour.

It did not always work, but every day I tried to have some time to myself, and I often managed quite a decent rest. Indeed I do not know how anyone manages without. However it is no good trying to escape interruptions altogether. Especially the more ingenious

28

ones.

Oliver, the last of the line, was still at home with me when everyone else had started school. He and I were in the garden one sunny afternoon. I could feel sleep closing in, but he wanted to read a little to me, and have me read a good bit to him. I agreed, on condition that when we had finished reading I would be allowed to shut myself up for a good rest. 'Oh, yes!' he said, he would have school with Teddy. I had been lying down for about ten minutes, and was just dropping off, when there was a tap at the door.

'Oliver! You promised you'd let me have a rest.'

'Yes, Mama. But surely you want to see Teddy's report!'

# Chapter 4
# 'LISTEN TO ME READING!'

WE DID not think of our first attempts at early reading as experiments. We were just trying to copy what we understood had worked for Montessori. We had read about Montessori's wish to have large wooden letters made. The prohibitive cost of these pushed her to the expedient of cutting similar letters out of sandpaper and sticking them on card. Her children were encouraged to run their fingers over the sandpaper letter as if they were writing it, sounding it at the same time, and in a short time they *were* writing. This led to reading, and it appeared that sandpaper letters at four suited most children.

We, at this stage, had a girl of three, a boy of about twenty-one months, and a baby of six months. The older two had been buttoning, building towers and stairs, fitting or filling insets, listening to rattley boxes for a short spell every day since before they could remember. They were up off the floor, able to sit on chairs at the table, and Barbara had begun to enjoy tracing patterns from Marion Richardson's *Writing and Writing Patterns*.

We got a couple of sheets of sandpaper and cut out capital letters two inches high, small enough to fit on a postcard. I have since learned that Montessori's first letters were small letters, designed to produce joined handwriting. However, in blissful ignorance of that, we offered the letters to three-year-old Barbara, following the Three Steps Method.

First I would feel the sandpaper 'M', up, down, up, down, with my middle finger, saying 'mmm'.

Then I would do the same with 'sss'.

Second step was 'Show me "mmm"' and 'Show me "sss"'.

The third step was to ask Barbara what each one was. It was no trouble to her to answer. She just was not interested. After all, she had been tracing patterns made of the same shapes, and I had been referring to them in the same way. Choice came into play, and Barbara chose not to be interested in the little card-shapes.

Alsadar at twenty-one months took a different attitude. Somehow he got the notion that something interesting was going on and he wanted to be in on it. He picked up one sound after another. He was not inclined to follow the example of feeling the letters, but he identified them confidently. I can remember, just after his second birthday, that the two of us were on the floor inside the door of the living-room. If it had been 'lesson' time we would have been at a table, or sitting on a rug, so this must have been an odd moment of enthusiasm. We had a blank sheet of paper and a pencil. I have an instant replay of the moment:

I write a large D. He says 'Duh'.

I write A. He says 'Ah'.

I point quickly, first to one, then to the other, and he says the sounds in quick succession.

'Da.'

I ask excitedly, 'What did you say, "DA"?'

At once I write the rest of DADA and he says the whole word.

Once Alasdar had the idea of running sounds into each other, it was easy to add new words. We were doing this before he was familiar with the whole alphabet. The second stage of his introduction to reading was the result of another lucky find. Just when we were ready for it the magazine *Housewife* published an article by someone who had found a way to help a child who was having difficulty reading. We began to play the game suggested when Alasdar knew about twenty letters, and he enjoyed it so much that we were kept busy night after night adding new sets of words.

Each set required twelve cards. Plain postcards are suitable. We had to think of six short words that named familiar objects and which used the letter-sounds.

Short, hard letter-sounds must be explained. Many other languages have just one sound to match each letter, and they even call the letter by that sound. This is why Italian and Spanish children can learn to read within three months of starting school, and many learn before school. The English language confronts children with two problems; letters and letter combinations can have several different sounds — you know the famous variations of 'ough' in bough, bought, rough, etc. As well as that, we are accustomed to giving some of the letters of the alphabet names that do not correspond to any of their sounds; neither 'G' in Gun nor 'G' in General sound like Gee.

It is possible to give English-speaking children as simple a start as Italians by settling on a frequently used sound for each letter and presenting mainly words that use those sounds until the knack of reading has been mastered. These more frequent sounds are the *short* sounds of the vowels: A, E, I, O, U, and the *hard* sounds of C and G. Here is a list of words showing short, hard sounds: AT BAG CUP DIP EGG FUN HUG IT JUMP KISS LEG MAN POP QUIX RUN SNAP TAP VAN WET YES ZIP. If the words Granny, Teddy or Daddy and Mummy are important, you will have to break the news that Y has two sounds.

Some people insist that it is not possible to sound a consonant by itself; that we must not teach simply 'D' but DA, DE, DI and so on. I can only say that I have never found any difficulty in making a sound which is somewhere between 'DUH' and 'DEH' and which *works* when it comes to blending sounds.

The first set of cards we made had pictures of Dada's HAT, Mama's Spanish FAN, Tinu's COT, a JUG, a PEG and a PIG, of the sort you meet in nursery rhymes. Note that PEG and PIG were put in to make sure Alasdar knew what he was doing. We drew matching hats on a pair of cards, matching fans, and so on; on the lower part of each card we wrote the word in capital letters. Six cards were left complete, the six matching cards had the words cut off.

He was given the set of complete cards, encouraged to set them out on the floor side by side. Then he was given the pictures alone, one picture being placed under the matching card. Would he guess that he was expected to put the others in place? Yes, he did. The next thing was to give him one of the words, suggest that he might read it. It said F A N. Where would it go? He got it right; under the picture of a fan. Here I was inspired to start a habit which was most helpful. I picked up the word and showed him that it matched, letter for letter, the word on the complete card. The advantage of checking in this way was that when he was playing by himself he might accidentally put PIG under the peg; this check made the material as nearly as possible self-correcting. The further advantage was that the children who learnt in this way became remarkably reliable at spelling.

Years later Alasdar had to attend a school where the leather strap was much used to punish error. Only once did the master find an excuse to use it on him in connection with spelling. Alasdar was asked to spell 'missile' and spelt 'missal'. The master did not disguise his satisfaction at having caught him out.

Our only problem with this spelling/reading game was to think of and draw suitable sets of words. We used coloured pencils — nowadays fibre pens give far better, clearer pictures. The words we used emerged from the interplay between the sounds we found ourselves needing and the young reader's available experience. Three-letter-words included EGG, CUP, GUN, VAN and BUS. When we needed to move on, double 'O' seemed an easily recognisable introduction to the idea that two letters together might have a sound of their own. For practice with OO we offered Alasdar his own three-legged STOOL, a nursery-rhyme MOON, a SPOON, a HOOP and, by way of illustrating a contrast, a picture of somebody standing on one leg with HOP underneath.

Then we tried OW. Seán had just made a toy TOWN for the children, and a picture of it worked well. We had COW, OWL, TOWER and WORDS. For the latter, we used a drawing of little slips with words on them, just like those the player was using.

Next came what proved to be favourites. We had pictures of the children's own clothes, and words like DRESS, SHIRT, SOCK, SANDAL and COAT. We did not notice that the word coat contains a sound that is neither O nor OO. The encouraging thing is that the reader did not notice either. He just recognised a familiar garment and linked it with letter sounds that came near enough. We did, however, realise that the SH in shirt was something new. The sound by itself, finger to lips, was familiar. We gave it much practice, with SHIP, SHOP, DISH, BRUSH and SPLASH. The next step was CHURCH, from the toy town again. CHAIR, WITCH, CLOCK and STICK followed.

A set of colours was easy to make, using coloured paper gummed onto the cards. PINK, RED and YELLOW ensued. The ow sound at the end of YELLOW is not exactly the same as in OWL, but the adjustment is easy.

Frequent games with these cards over a whole year must have laid a solid foundation for reading. The next landmark came when Alasdar was three-and-a-quarter.

We were sitting near the kitchen window, the light shining on the pages of Brown and Nolan's *First Reader*. Sean brought it home because there were only a few lines on each page, the print was clear, and there was a picture of a bus we knew well, the number 44. I waited to see what he would make of the first page. In fact, he continued with it for the whole morning, must have allowed me to make lunch and give some attention to Barbara and Tinu, but was determined to finish the little book that day. Only one word gave him any bother — 'high'.

The particularly intriguing aspect of this feat is that the book was all in lower case, with capitals at the beginning of the sentences in the ordinary way — while the cards from which he had learnt had nothing but capitals.

The next obvious step was to find the second book, but as it had not, at the time, been printed, we made do with Beacon Readers, which had well-planned phonic word lists at the back of each volume. When, for various reasons to be explained later, Alasdar went to a Montessori School at three-and-three-quarters, he was reading independently, and the whole planned progression of sandpaper letters, movable letters and sets of words matched with objects had nothing to offer him. Instead, he concentrated on filling in geometric insets. His model insets were still in evidence years after he left school.

When he was five years and two months old we shared a railway carriage with the headmaster of a boys' preparatory school. Alasdar spent some of the time absorbed in *Robin*, an exceptionally good children's comic, then at its peak. Eventually the school-master spoke.

'Is he really reading it?'

Alasdar was asked to demonstrate, and did. This was the first time it was suggested to me that it was at all out of the way for a five-year-old (much less a four-year-old) to be reading at sight, silently. The encounter sowed some seeds of suspicion regarding the achievements of the school system.

While observing Alasdar's progress I had learned something of the irregularity of English spelling, and was grateful for Beacon Readers, which sorted words into groups which made them much easier to assimilate than the same words would have been, encountered at random. I also learned that reading along with a small child is very enjoyable.

The surprise was that Barbara was not finding it enjoyable. She would most often choose some other occupation, drawing, insets, tracing or sorting out sounds, in preference to anything related to reading. Of course, she liked to be read *to* as much as anyone else. It would have been absurd to insist that a four-year-old *must* read. Anyway, I did not go in for insisting on anything. It would also have been tactless to expose her to competition with her younger brother, as the gap between them in this particular skill continued to increase. I just hoped that the writing involved in her tracing books — the charming sentences and verses chosen by Marion Richardson — would keep her sufficiently in touch with reading.

Eventually, by the time she was six, we felt we had better insist that she spend a little time reading with Séan in the evening. Even then she dug her heels in about doing the lists at the back of the book, so that she was still quite a slow reader at seven and a wonderfully imaginative speller at seventeen.

I now realise that some of her problems had a suggestion of dyslexia about them, but that had not then been heard of. Barbara did not have three-dimensional capital letters as early as the others, she had them on the flat instead; she was tracing small letters as well as capitals before she had learnt to read, and she did not meet the whole thing as early as the others did. It should have worked. It did not.

When it came to the turn of Tinu, who was fifteen months younger than Alasdar, and Janet, a year and nine months younger again, I did not make those mistakes. I knew from Alasdar's progress that I was on the right track. On the other hand, I had seen some proper sandpaper letters and knew that mine were not at all the thing. But these authentic Montessori versions, designed to develop *writing*, were hardly attractive for a two-year-old. Plastic capital letters, costing a few pence in Woolworths, on the other hand, were successful objects for the Three Steps Method.

Having got my letters, I was prudent enough not to hand over the whole alphabet at once. I started Tinu with her own letter, T. As soon as she could be counted on to say 'tuh' when she saw T, and 'sss' when she saw S, I offered T and O together. Because the plastic letters were movable, it was easy to nudge two of them closer and closer together, to indicate that the sounds should come closer together, too. DA became DADA, MA became MAMA.

When reading Michael Deakin's *The Children on the Hill* (Andre Deutsch) I was fascinated to note that the infinitely energetic Montessori mother in the book intended to make sandpaper letters for her children, but her two-and-a-half-year-old son spotted plastic capitals in a shop window, persuaded her to buy them and, it seems, knew half of them by evening and began to make words.

Games with letters (demonstrating KISS, HUG and JUMP) moved smoothly into games with the cards we had made for Alasdar. We added new sets from time to time and found the lists in the Beacon Readers very helpful. Realising that Alasdar's jump from cards in capitals to a book in lower-case letters could not be expected again, we inserted three extra stages.

The new picture cards had words written in one corner in lower case, as well as more prominently in capitals. At the same time, the children began to use the *Writing Pattern* books, which made them more familiar with lower case. I made small cards with a capital letter in the middle, a print lower-case to one side, a handwriting version on the other. When we looked at them I tried to show that lower-case letters were really capitals written quickly.

Even from there I did not move straight into real books. For Janet, who came after Tinu, and for Pierce, Thomas, Rebecca, Eoin and Oliver, I made their own little books, using small spiral-backed sketch books, easy to handle and to fill. Durable too — some of them survive today. A typical couple of pages have such factual entries as:

JANET GOT A MUSHROOM. SHE PUT IT IN THE PAN FOR DADA. HE PUT SALT ON IT AND HAD IT FOR DINNER. SHE HAD FISH AND PUT LEMON ON IT.

We walked around difficult sounds. The early books would never have a phrase like THOMAS CLIMBS THE BEECH TREE. The younger children would not know about silent B in climbs. He went up instead.

This sort of simplification becomes instinctive when you are writing for children whose progress you are involved with all the time, as opposed to a class, handed on by some other teacher.

It has been suggested that puzzling out lists of words with similar spelling, as in the Beacon phonetic lists, is just the sort of work from which little children should be protected. However, we found it to be like many other things that take on the colour of drudgery at a later age, for instance polishing shoes. For a three or four year-old child, it seems a thoroughly agreeable exercise of a recently acquired skill. Only Barbara disliked the drill we established, of going through lists of words with key sounds in them before reading a Beacon Reader story. The others took the list-reading before the story quite for granted, since it only lasted a few minutes. It was important that they were reading because they pestered me to listen, not because I was chasing them, or because it was time for a class to read. In fact, it was at this stage, when the reader was about four, that I was most in demand. One after another, the children found that they could make out stories for themselves. He or she would call me three or four times a day.

'Listen to me reading!'

The sessions usually lasted twenty minutes — longer if we were anxious to finish a story. Four years of age was average. Alasdar reached this point at three. Thomas, from the evidence of his home-made book, was still at the capital stage at age four. However, he was always an outdoor chap and, although he knew the letters, had little interest in working out words until one day when he proudly showed me a bird in a nest that he had made out of modelling clay.

When I had admired the work I wrote BIRD NEST TWIG WING and EGG on a handy card and his interest was captured. Once he found out that there were books written about birds, there was some point in learning to read.

This early start at an age when children are interested in naming things and associating sounds with letters, gave us plenty of time and made the whole process most agreeable. In our daily lessons, reading was one choice. We also read to the children at every bed-time, even long after they could read to themselves. Often the bed-time session meant a competent reader listening while one of us was reading to the younger ones. If there were an unexpected interruption the parent might come back to find that the elder brother or sister had gone on with the story.

Again, there was no question of leaving them on their own as soon as they had attained silent reading, which usually happened about six weeks after the first demands to 'listen to me reading'. Some reading aloud continued to be a normal part of lessons for a good while. Every now and again I would reassert the necessity of going over the phonic tables. Pierce, the seventh child, was going on for six when I did this.

'We don't seem to have done any "back of the book" for ages. Try this page and I'll help you with the hard ones.'

'Which hard ones? Symphony? Determination?'

# Chapter 5
# THE SECOND HOUSE

IN TIME, there were five children in the house on the hill; Barbara, Alasdar, Tinu, Janet and Claire. And after five years we were no longer so isolated. One of the families farming half-way down had a little girl slightly older than Barbara, so she could have guided Barbara to the nearest National School. However, by that time, we had read the report of a Commission on Primary Education and as a result we were doubtful about the likely benefits.

Then Pat and Luan Cuffe built themselves a house in the wood and moved in, together with their two children who overlapped in age with ours. Having discovered not so long beforehand that there was an Irish Montessori Society meeting monthly in Dublin, we introduced the Cuffes to the idea. They were impressed, entered their children in a Children's House in Stillorgan and offered to bring any of ours we wanted to send. The directress would not accept Barbara, because, at five, she was too old. We sent Alasdar, then nearly four, and Tinu, fifteen months younger, who had the longest spell there, spending almost a year in the place. After one term Janet, not yet three, took Alasdar's place and had a couple of terms before we moved house.

We were much impressed on our arrival at the school, the first morning of the post-Christmas term. All the children were moving around independently, picking out their selected material and getting down to work, so that the two directresses were quite free to welcome newcomers and talk to Pat Cuffe and myself. The activity, the order, the housekeeping all demonstrated that what Montessori had said was true. The experience was most helpful to us even after we moved house, because it encouraged Tinu and Janet to believe that a time spent learning was a normal part of everyone's morning.

On the other hand, while the organisation and observation that kept some sixty children working independently was very much to be admired, the skill was needed mainly because there were so many children together. It was not certain that the individual children were getting better value than the small group at home.

During the summer of the year that Tinu spent at the Children's House I was persuaded by my father, who had retired to a good-sized flat in Galicia in Spain, to bring the children out for a holiday. While there, in the hope that they might pick up some Spanish, I sent Barbara, Alasdar and Tinu to school. The attempt was a failure. Tinu remembers one nun holding an apple up over her head saying 'Manzana, manzana', in an attempt to get Tinu to repeat the word. All Tinu would say was 'Naughty nun, naughty nun', while jumping up and down to get the apple.

Barbara learned to do fine embroidery. It was probably the only thing the nuns could think of doing with the little foreigner. The skill undoubtedly helped to get her off to an early start with dressmaking.

Tinu, although she learned very little Spanish, must nonetheless have established some form of communication with her classmates, because she told me that she was tired of being asked whether she was a girl or not. All female babies in those parts used to have ear-rings inserted sometime in the first week of life and are never seen without them afterwards. She was to have her fourth birthday in July, in the middle of our three-month stay, and I promised her a pair of ear-rings. On the day, we went to a jeweller in the town and selected a pair of 'sleepers', the tiny unobtrusive ear-rings worn all the time. The jeweller, who was in the habit of pushing the point of the sleeper through a baby's unresisting ear, took Tinu's earlobe and shoved. There was a bellow of pain, a spurt of blood, splashing tears. Then the head was turned, of its own accord, to have the other ear adorned.

It was in the winter following the Spanish holiday that we recognised we could hardly stay on the hill forever. Five children were a tight fit. An inevitable sixth would make it tighter. Water was a continuing problem. We were discussing the possibility of digging a well when the news came that the railway on which we relied was to be closed.

We began to look for alternatives, and Sean went to look at a house in Rathfarnham because the description mentioned that the ground rent was one peppercorn. We never found out to whom we should pay the peppercorn, but the Mill House suited us perfectly.

It was large and country Georgian, built in 1810. It had a big warm kitchen with tiled walls and floor, a bathroom with a bath large enough to hold all five children at once, and a garden that was a safe suntrap.

On the east it was separated from the road by a bank, a hedge and the old mill-stream, and on the west by a wall running the whole length of the garden, the only entrance being a panelled iron door in the wall with a handle too high for a child to reach. There were trees — willow, elm, ash, two copper beeches — and a mass of elder bushes crowded the bank. The house itself faced due south, so that quite often, sitting on the stone bench between the windows, I have been fooled into thinking we were enjoying a really hot day when elsewhere there was a cutting wind.

We added pear trees, raspberries, a morello cherry, and a scrap of rosemary which is now a spreading bush where pillowcases dry smelling of incense. There was a scruffy wilderness at the south end of the garden, which Tinu cleared, planting instead daffodils, peonies, fritillaries and hellebores.

For the children, the bank offered scope for hide and seek or solitary play. Then there was the pool in the mill-stream into which they used to fall summer after summer. How many small shoes have floated away down that stream!

We hung a twenty-foot rope from one of the limbs of the otherwise inaccessible copper beech, and we have a photograph of Rebecca well up the rope at the age of three. Right beside the copper beech, within reach of the rope, there was a laburnum that had grown sideways instead of upward. That unfortunate plant has often had a dozen children swarming on it, either hanging by their knees or taking turns jumping from the laburnum onto the rope. There was a swing, and a sandpit. With possibilities like these you do not have to look for a play group. It finds you.

This used to be a problem during the mornings of the school holidays, when the new acquaintances would turn up at ten o'clock and distract someone who was engaged in lessons. I tried to involve the more regular callers in what was going on, but they were not as used as the family were to working on their own and I had neither the time nor the skill to convert them. Unless we started very early we did not get much done, although there were built-in advantages to our system. Someone who had just found that she could read would follow me around regardless of how many children played in the garden.

Things, then, went on as before, but more conscientiously. We now had five students, and we had made a great deal of our own materials, including addition and subtraction boards and short multiplication tables to go with beads. (See *Resources*).

For the two youngest, Janet, then aged four, and Claire, going on for two, we were lucky enough to get a proper set of Montessori cylinders.

We got ourselves a handsome globe for geography, and we used the sandpit in the garden to illustrate islands, peninsulas and melting ice. They could appreciate the effect of heavy rain on our own stream. Particularly appreciated was *Collins Progressive Atlas*, which begins with a picture of 'John's house' as seen from the air, then a map to match the picture, then another photograph from higher up, and another map, until the aerial view moves far enough up to take in the whole world. This implied the possibility of making maps of our own schoolroom, and garden. I was surprised to find that this can fascinate even a three-year-old.

Three and four year-olds got great value out of Waddington's 'simple jigsaws of the world', with four or five pieces to each continent with pictures of suitable beasts or monuments. It was easy to find simple books talking about other countries, houses, food, climate and people. When we had matching music, we would put on a record. I remember reading a Japanese tale about a little chap who was found in a peach. The book was printed in Japan, and we would arrange a set of Japanese dolls to listen in.

For history, we made four wall charts, a thousand years each with ten lines of a hundred years ruled across. We stuck small pictures on whenever we had been talking about historical events or figures. A Botticelli Madonna and child marked the junction between B.C. and A.D. There was a harp at about 1000 B.C. for David, a ram at about 2000 B.C. for Abraham. When we read about Hannibal crossing the Alps someone drew an elephant to stick on around 200 B.C. St. Patrick's fire at Slane was placed around A.D. 400. At 1810 a picture of our second house appeared, and in recent years the names of each member of the family were added as they appeared.

One subject I am sorry we dropped was Latin. Sean had come across *Latin with Laughter* by Sidney Frankenberg (out of print). She had written it for her six year-old son in order to make easier his initiation into Latin at the age of eight in a prep school, and so it also suited Alasdar, at the same age. The Latin words were written on slips of cardboard with tiny drawings if needed, and the case endings were separate letters. With these slips, it was very easy to make up the Latin sentences suggested and write them into a copy. They are all about sailors being stung by wasps and queens being chased by goats. Alasdar got enormous fun out of it and used to constantly call on me to do some Latin with him. I did not introduce the other children to this book, because I found that they would not meet Latin until post-primary school and I thought it would all be forgotten. This proved not to be the case with Alasdar, and the others might well have benefited from an early acquaintance; what a pity I did not know about Esperanto then.

At this time too we discovered BBC Radio, finding that we could not only listen to Schools Programmes about science, pre-history and other subjects, but we could get a list of the year's plan and write away for illustrated booklets to back them up. Aidan especially was devoted to these programmes, and everyone joined in with 'Music and Movement' from early on.

Ronald Ridout's *English Workbooks* were the most useful aid to independent work for different ages. Their merit is that all the information needed to work out a page correctly is on that page, provided the child is at the right level. This makes it easy to succeed. They focus the child's attention on things they would hardly notice for themselves, like singular and plural, alphabetical order and the advantages of telling a story from beginning to end. At the same time they make it possible for an adult to correct mistakes without bruising anyone's creative enthusiasm.

# Chapter 6
## 'THAT'S NOT CHILD ART . . .'

PAINTING began early, was a constant interest for perhaps three-quarters of the family progress and has so far had a considerable share in three careers.

There was a great expansion of this activity when we moved to the Mill House and found white-tiled kitchen walls ready for Barbara, Tinu and Janet to paint on. Alasdar preferred paper, but Claire, aged eighteen months, was only the first of the toddlers to paint on a lower section, while her elders worked away over her head. I used to give each baby one colour first, usually yellow, which did not do so much damage when spilt on clothes. This was mixed in small quantities in a jam jar. Progress would be made to two colours side by side on a saucer, to be gradually blended while they painted.

I was careful not to ask too many questions. Children often find out what they are painting by looking at it, rather than by planning first. There is a regular sequence. Zigzags and circular scribbles are followed by circles with indications of eyes and mouth, plus arms and legs. All children seem to go through these stages if they are given the chance to draw. Our batch seemed to reach each stage rather sooner than average, no doubt as a natural outcome of beginning early. I have always been delighted to watch a small child painting, the sure little hand holding the brush six or seven inches from the tip, watching so carefully, one length of the line just as important as another, the child totally wrapped up in creation.

I remember a delightful one of Oliver's, when he was about two-and-a-half. He started off, using dark sugar paper, with two parallel lines moving across the centre from the bottom left-hand corner. Then short lines across these, like a ladder. Next a yellow shape and a scatter of yellow dots.

He went off and left the picture. An hour or so later, when I was thinking of tidying it away, he hurried in, took a brush and black paint and added some large squares each divided into four.

'Now it's the Moon and windows and a ladder to the stars.'

Of all the treasures I have lost to Caltex, I think that is the one I regret most. If I had had any notion that the artist was going to retire quite soon, I would never have parted with it.

The oil company Caltex, later known as Texaco, sponsored an annual art competition which was a quite important event for us over a period of thirteen years. One day when Tinu was about seven she painted rapidly on the kitchen wall a woman kneeling, one arm supporting her, the other stretched out to pull a carrot. It must have been me. I knew it would have to be washed off the wall sometime, so I asked her to try to paint something like it on paper. It came out pretty well. Then I saw a notice of this competition, and sent it in.

Tinu won a tennis racquet and we were hooked. Glen Abbey Textiles ran a competition of the same sort. In the following year we sent off a bundle of paintings to each of them. Over the next thirteen years, two, three or four of the children won something in either or both contests. I had misgivings about becoming involved in competition, but the standard did become visibly higher and higher, and esteem for painting was encouraged.

The record year is noted in the Birthday Book.

We shall hardly do better than this year. Barbara, Janet, Thomas and Rebecca all won prizes in Caltex. Barbara won first prize and Rebecca was the youngest winner. She was also the subject of the painting that won the first prize, so she was on the cover of a magazine the Government sends out to different countries. Barbara won first prize in Glen Abbey, too, with a picture of Tinu holding Oliver. Janet won a bicycle from Pink Paraffin as well for drawing.

The following year, Janet took top place in Caltex and top in her age group in Glen Abbey. In Barbara's winning year she also collected an award in an adult contest which allowed her six months' use of the facilities for etching and lithography in the Graphic Studio. Since the child art competition, Caltex and Glen Abbey, claimed 30,000 entries each, it was not unreasonable for both Barbara and Janet to think of careers in that field. Tinu took a dislike to the fuss of competitions at a fairly early stage, after winning each time she entered, and continued her own way drawing flowers.

Whatever damage may have been done by competitiveness was probably outweighed by the experience of not winning — of taking the rough with the smooth.

When Thomas was eight or nine he had already been devoted to birds for several years. One day he came home quite excited and wanted paper and paint at once, to paint a swan he had seen when he was crossing over the canal. I found a piece of black paper. With a few strokes of white, some green reeds in front, he produced a bird of oriental economy. When the time for Caltex came around, I felt so sure the swan would get a prize, and therefore be available for collection afterwards, that I risked sending it off. Sure enough, Thomas was one of the prizewinners, but for a different painting.

Having been invited to the press reception, I asked one of the judges if he remembered seeing a white swan on a black ground. Yes, he remembered it well. It had struck him particularly.

'Why was it the other one that got the prize, then?'

'Well, the swan wasn't really child art . . . .'

So we never got our swan back. But every year about twenty children in each age-group, and a proportion of teachers and parents, were invited to lunch at the Gresham Hotel in Dublin for the prize-giving, and quite a few turned up year after year and had an agreeable day out.

I had no guilt about encouraging them to enter for handwriting competitions, in which they won numbers of prizes over a period of about six years. The *Sunday Independent* had a competition in which competitors were asked to write a fairly long passage in prose, and this paid off, not only in lastingly good handwriting but in pocket money and fountain pens.

Like Thomas, Rebecca, who at eight was drawing better than anyone had done before, found an animal love and became obsessed with it as a subject. With Rebecca it was horses. From twelve onwards she would draw nothing else.

One change in our approach to drawing and painting came accidentally. An uncle of mine died and left me an unexpected legacy. With this windfall we started to tidy up the house. The new wallpaper was too good to have drawing-pins stuck in it, so the frieze of paintings that had been changing, but always full, disappeared. The fine big Nativity collage Barbara had organised the others to do when she was fourteen was not pinned up the Christmas after the legacy. The kitchen was modernised with a dishwasher and kitchen units. This did not stop anyone painting on the wall, but the fact that I was not spending so much time at a sink, and therefore was less readily available for mixing paint, had some influence.

The table, ten feet long, topped with white marble, had always been a surface which tempted pencils. It was perpetually covered with drawing, and I used to find myself washing around the best ones. Now, post-legacy, it was covered with a tablecloth which unfortunately protected it from pencils.

Painting and drawing were somewhat discouraged for the younger end of the family when Oliver was going on for three and we were joined by David, whose mother asked if he could share lessons with us. Suddenly many things, painting included, became more formal. The boys would get everything ready in the morning, but wait till David arrived before starting lessons. Oliver was less likely to begin a painting, walk off from it, and come back when he knew what he wanted. Whatever the reasons, from about the time that Oliver turned three, the stream of creativity that used to ripple through the house, leaving sediment on its banks, now flows no more than intermittently.

What painting may have lost music may have gained. If I were able to return to the beginning I would see that every child had a chance to learn to play an instrument, just as every child had a chance to learn to read. Perhaps early music is more important than early mathematics or, indeed, facts of any kind. Everything else can be picked up fairly easily from twelve onwards, but it is frustrating in the teens and twenties to want to play something and be held up for lack of the dexterity that could have been built in by early practice and parental foresight.

We had no money for tuition; I cannot play a note, Séan had only had lessons for two years and did not feel qualified to teach anyone. But at least we had the piano, and Séan was engaged in teaching himself some Tudor pieces from the *Fitzwilliam Virginal Book*, so Barbara had enough example to teach herself how to read music from one of those diagrams that stretch along the keyboard.

That was when she was under seven — before the move. Later Barbara took piano lessons, thanks to a kind aunt, and did regular exams getting 97 per cent or 98 per cent each time. She picked up

46

theory particularly fast. The Leaving Certificate, however, left no time to spare for music.

Alasdar was given a mouth-organ in his Christmas stocking when he was five, and was able to play recognisable tunes on it right away. He even knew, quite soon, which ones he should *not* play because of the limitations of the instrument. With each succeeding birthday he was given progressively better mouth-organs, and they became a social asset as well as pleasure. When he was twelve (and planning to be a pilot) he used to cycle out to the military airport, where he was most hospitably welcomed, allowed to explore instrument panels, given meals in the canteen, and encouraged to play for his supper.

As soon as he had earned himself enough money he bought himself a guitar, then better guitars, and it is his frustration at not being Julian Bream or John Williams that makes me wish I could start over again.

Things were simpler for Tinu, because her voice is her instrument. It used to be marvellous to hear through the house.

'He brak his fiddle aboun' his knee . . .'

or

'Waly, waly up the bank
And waly, waly, doun the brae . . . .'

Later folk gave way to traditional jazz and Tinu sang seriously with a group. However, if they did not get sufficient chances to play music when they were younger, at least they listened. 'Music and Movement' on BBC Radio was a big favourite as soon as we had a radio, which was at the time Tinu, the third child, was born. There was the piano and, after the move, a record player. When they were young, they each had a special record.

Barbara's 'own' record was Dvorak's 'New World Symphony'; Alasdar's Sousa's marches. Tinu used to whirl around to Katachurian's 'Sabre Dance'. Janet chose some Peer Gynt, plus 'Night on a Bare Mountain' which I believe conjures up a gathering of witches. Claire had some dances from 'The Bartered Bride' by Smetana, while Aidan owned 'Three German Dances', little scraps of Mozart. Pierce's was 'Elizabethan Serenade', a change from all those Slav or German pieces, but Thomas went further into Russia with a camel train advancing and fading away over 'The Steppes of Central Asia'. Everyone enjoyed French folk songs.

Alasdar now plays Bach and Segovia on the classical guitar, quite a step from Souza; Aidan is devoted to playing jazz, both of them wish they were more proficient. The three youngest were given a better chance, piano lessons for Rebecca and Oliver from a most sympathetic teacher who did not believe in being dominated by exams, while Eoin was encouraged by his headmaster to study the violin, so that he sould think more carefully about what he was doing. He, too, had an exceptionally good teacher, but none of the three wished to continue when, for different reasons, their teachers moved away. Rebecca is the only one of the youngest who plays a little from time to time.

# Chapter 7
# READING:
# ORTHODOXY AND DOMAN

ONE INDICATION of the new attitude to learning that was linked with the move to a new house was my resolve to use correct methods in teaching the younger children to read. We had provided ourselves with the full set of Beacon Readers, including a thick Teacher's Book, and I learnt that what we had been doing so far was not right. It was too late to do anything about the first four, but Claire was only eighteen months old at the time of the move, so she could have a proper introduction.

The method described was the very opposite to ours. Instead of beginning with capital letters, we should apparently have started with whole sentences and worked down slowly to letters. 'Kitty has the ball', then one little box saying 'Kitty has', and another little box saying 'the ball'. When the student had worked through the book about Kitty and Rover she should be familiar with thirty 'sight words', and then we could point out which letter was associated with which sound.

Claire was an amiable child, and she co-operated. But I got bored, turning back the pages of 'Kitty' to show her where she had already met the word or the sentence that was baffling her. She progressed through the other readers, but much more slowly than Tinu and Janet, and without ever insisting, 'Listen to me reading'.

When Aidan's turn came I had not entirely lost faith in the Beacon Teacher's Book, but I modified the approach by telling him about letter sounds at the same time as we began with the sentences and the flash cards. We had a set of large plastic lower-case letters, and our own set of sandpaper letters.

Aidan did not complain either, but some spark seemed to be missing. Both Claire and Aidan started later than the others, because it did not seem reasonable to offer a printed book to children under two. Indeed, I do not remember what age they were when they were introduced to 'Kitty and Rover', but I found long afterwards (when I was sorting through records in order to put this book together) that both of them had been aged seven when they were doing the same Ridout *'English Workbook'* that Janet before them and Rebecca after them had done when barely five.

By the time Pierce was a year old I had decided that old ways were best; we returned comfortably to our early Three-Dimensional Capitals. It was gratifying to find that both Pierce and Rebecca moved just as smoothly through the several stages; letters, cards, home-made books, Beacon Readers, on to anything in print. Thomas was distracted by his outdoor interests, but he learnt very quickly once he found that print might contain information about birds.

When Eoin's turn came, there was a bit of a hitch. He had not yet begun to speak when he had reached the age of two and a quarter. It had not been possible to use the 'Three Steps' before he was two. About the same time I read an article by Glenn Doman in *The Ladies Home Journal.* He said that babies can, like to and should be allowed to read. Of course I agreed. In this article he suggested that familiar words written on cards in large red capital letters should be shown to the child briefly once or twice a day. He stressed that it was a way to have fun together.

I had already tried whole words, but this was not quite the same. Doman was persuasive, and Eoin's case was special. I kept the idea in mind. Then one day something exciting happened. As I came up the garden path I noticed that my silent toddler was sitting on the grass whispering to himself. He was repeating part of the family night prayers, 'God bless Mama and Dada, Barbara and Alasdar and Tinu and Janet and Claire and Aidan and Pierce and Thomas and Rebecca and Eoin and Oliver.'

I went quietly in, found a large red marker and cut four strips of white cardboard at least eight inches high. On them I wrote in large capitals MAMA, JANET, EOIN, AIDAN. When he wandered in, I was waiting. I sat him on my knee and showed him two of the cards, using the old Three Steps. When I asked him to 'Show me MAMA?', 'Show me AIDAN?', he got them right. Said them too. Then he noticed that I had two more cards under my arm. He wanted to see them. I told him these two names as well, and he got these right also. We were both very pleased with ourselves. I put the cards up on a shelf.

Next morning Eoin came down to breakfast. He looked up, saw the ends of his cards sticking out over the edge, indicated that he wanted them. Took one from my hand, said 'Mama — no, Janet'. And it *was* Janet. He then said the right name for each of the other three. I was staggered.

Of course we continued. For some weeks we added one or two words every day. There was a break while we had friends staying and when we came back to our words Eoin remembered thirty of them. Oliver, at fifteen months, was delighted to have a card with his favourite word BIRDY written on it.

The three of us had quite a lot of fun laying out long sentences about worms having hot baths and snails jumping. The trouble began when each had a sight vocabulary of about 130 words including at least as many words in lower case as in capitals. I had by that time taught them the letter-sounds (as Doman recommends in his book *Teach Your Baby to Read*).

Even so, when they began to get mixed up between words that look alike, they did *not* want to go back and sort out the problem. They were accustomed to words signalling their meaning at a glance; they resented the need to back-track, and were prepared to settle for whatever came into their heads first. Oliver went on strike at the age of three; he would get me to read to him but when it was his turn he would be 'too tired'. You can hardly tell a three-year-old that that is not fair. As for Eoin, he went on making wild guesses.

On the gain side of Glenn Doman's method there was plenty of fun, but there was enjoyment with the early capital letters, too. On the loss side the readers were not nearly so independent, they did not lay a sound foundation for spelling, and they became gradually more confused instead of finding things clearer and clearer. A major difficulty was that when they were reading alone, *they did not know that they did not know.* If they were reading aloud, a listener could call a halt and say, 'Have another look at that?'

The child reading alone would settle for some familiar word and carry on until confused and frustrated. A couple of mistakes, noted when the readers were aged seven and nine, were Badminington for Badminton, and Roger Lacely Green for Roger Lancely Green. True, these were proper names, but even so the readers should not have been happy to add or subtract a syllable.

As it turned out it was important that Eoin should have been taught to read early, and at home, by whatever method was chosen.

At one stage, when we were having IQ tests done, I brought himself and Oliver along and they came out neck-and-neck, both 'superior'. But it was remarked that, while Eoin's reading was in advance of his age, the kind of mistakes he made were similar to those made by deaf children. It was arranged that he should have a proper screening and it emerged that he was slightly deaf. I had twice brought him to Health Centre clinics and had been assured that his hearing was normal. If he had been left to learn in a class at school age, I think it likely that he would have been left far behind.

The Capital Letters

Aa Bb Cc Dd Ee

Ff Gg Hh Ii Jj

Kk Ll Mm Nn

Oo Pp Qq Rr Ss

Tt Uu Vv Ww

Xx Yy Zz

& Small Letters

# Chapter 8

# TEACHING OF NUMBER

THE TEACHING of number, on the other hand, began simply with counting things. We counted sausages, steps of stairs, daisies, jumps and biscuits. Jumps stopped at ten. When we came to thirteen and fourteen daisies, we pointed out that we were counting three-and-ten, four-and-ten, and that twenty and thirty were bundles of tens. We also tried to impress upon the small learners that this grouping of tens was just for convenience because of having ten fingers.

They were given to understand that other cultures had counted in sixes and that a variety of bases could be used equally conveniently. We were not warned that children should be taught in these terms, but the fact that it even occurred to me suggests that I had already looked at Tobias Dantzig's *Number, the Language of Science.*

There was meaning in even the simple counting. We counted daisies as we picked them. Three in one bunch. Five in the other. Which has more? What's the difference? I have noticed since then that parents who do not make a habit of such enquiry are inclined to believe that when their small children can count they know what they are saying, which is not necessarily the case.

There was opportunity everywhere. Eggs come in egg boxes, three one way, two the other, six altogether. Or they come in trays, five rows of six each. Cake papers have to be put into trays that hold either three or four rows of three. Fruit and sweets have to be divided fairly. One morning Dada gets four letters in the post while Mama gets two, or vice versa.

Oliver surprised me one morning. I had asked him to carry empty milk bottles out to the front door. He brought out two, then another two. When he came back, I asked him how many were outside now.

'Four,' he said.

'And if you bring this one out, how many will there be?

'Five, and if I had another there would be six.'

It may not sound much to an adult, but there had to be a fair amount of number conversation going on before a three-year-old could add a hypothetical milk bottle to four that are absent and one that is in the hand.

I took advantage of joint activities such as cooking. Anyone old enough to stand on a stool can add a teaspoonful of salt when called for. They can manage half and quarter-teaspoonfuls with measuring spoons, or, more excitingly, fill an ordinary teaspoon and divide the contents down the middle with a knife. If you are using an American cook book, you need half and quarter and one-third cups. If European, you measure in pints and half-pints, or litres and half-litres. This gives a chance to demonstrate that glass measuring jugs show more than one sort of measure, while the goblet of the liquidiser shows the pint and the half-litre. This can develop into measuring by spans and cubits and feet, or using the floor tiles as units for comparing the length of Teddy and his companions. But all of this had to wait until the mixing bowl was washed.

For the children's sake I provided myself with a scales using weights rather than a spring balance with a dial. The smaller children found it a challenge to work out how we would weigh six ounces when we only had weights labelled two, four and eight ounces. By the time they could think that one out, they could weigh things themselves, and even sift the flour through a sieve. Questions accompanied all of this activity. The packet of margarine was labelled 8 oz., but we need only four. Could the helper cut this off without using weights, or using them only to check? How about two ounces? Or six? The handy marble kitchen table gave us somewhere on which to write the number of divisions made and the number of corresponding segments used.

The need to increase quantities in proportion was a frequent exercise, as we always needed to make more than was said in the book. 'Serves four' meant we had to double, and eventually treble, the quantities.

The recipe said three ounces of fat, three of sugar, five of flour, one egg. If we used three eggs, how much fat and sugar did we need? When fifteen ounces of flour were decided upon, was there any short cut? We would agree that a pound of flour weighs sixteen ounces. We needed only fifteen. The task, then, was to get them into the bowl without pouring the whole lot onto the scales.

Of course, I did not go through all of that every time. If I had, cakes would have been rare. But we always did *something* besides licking the bowl. It might be practice in separating eggs, something which is more easily done when there is no real need, when a scrap of yolk in the white does not matter. Or it might be mixing vinegar and bread soda after making soda bread, watching them fizz, tasting them and learning the words 'acid' and 'alkali'.

It did slow cooking down a bit. Unhelped, I can have a round of brown bread in the oven two-and-a-half minutes after I have decided to make it. However, if a session on these lines had gone well we might not feel the need for anything further in the way of lessons. And we were doing the kind of things that primary schools now go to a good deal of trouble to bring into the classroom. It certainly was worth the time spent on it. Older girls often asked if they might make a cake as a distraction from prolonged study. Barbara used to make several Christmas cakes every year until I retired her at the age of twelve, to allow Tinu to take over.

When Eoin was six years old he asked me if he could make Granny's birthday cake. She was coming over for her party. I said certainly. He could buy anything he needed in the shop next door while I was up at the village — I would not be gone long.

I was not. When I came back I saw no signs of bags of flour or sugar; I asked him had he forgotten about the cake.

'No,' he said, 'It's in the oven, and it'll be done when the pinger sounds...'

The practical experience was tied in with theory. Just as the children had been given insets when they were a couple of years younger than they would have been in a Montessori school, so we provided 'the long stairs' at an early stage, and made number cards, strung beads together, and so on, copying what we read about. I shall not describe the Montessori material here; a few words in 'Resources' should be sufficient, because anyone who wishes to use it will find it described in detail in Dr Montessori's own books along with her penetrating reflections on the children's use of it. Certainly, it served us well; everyone who used it moved through school without difficulty, to say the least.

At some time in junior school Alasdar was asked why he was not saying tables. He was able to ask in turn, 'Have I ever got a sum wrong?' If I say nothing about this useful material, it is because halfway through the family, in time for Aidan and Pierce, I happened to see in a magazine an advertisement for the *Colour-Factor Set*. It sounded as if it might be an agreeable addition to the home-made material we had. I wrote off for the box of blocks and some books that went with them.

Colour-Factor Blocks were a revelation. I am glad to be able to say that the designer, Seton Pollock, acknowledged a debt to Montessori's Long Stairs, as well as to others who had used the same principle. The reason for using rods of different length is to help the learner understand that each natural number is not simply a bunch of units, more or less as the case may be, but that each has its own nature and combines with others accordingly. When seen in this way numbers are much more enjoyable to manipulate and the results of the manipulation are more clearly visible. They are visible not only to the student but also to any interested observer, who can almost see how the child is thinking, which is far from being the case when he is merely writing down figures.

Montessori's Long Stairs consisted of ten rods, the longest one metre long, marked off in sections of ten centimetres, the shortest, ten centimetres. The longest Colour-Factor Block is only twelve centimetres, the unit, a cube of one centimetre; they are all one centimetre through, just a little thicker than a pencil. As their name indicates, each has a different colour, relating to its factors. For example, the three-unit block is light blue, the nine-unit royal blue; when you range two sixes, three fours, four threes and six twos alongside the twelve-unit block it is not only obvious that each chain of one colour equals the twelve in length, but that blues (showing three as a factor) and reds (showing two as a factor) run through the pattern, converging in a darkish purple for twelve.

There are in one set enough blocks, twelve tens, twenty-four yellow fives, one-hundred-and-forty whites, to make possible quite elaborate patterns. Rebecca, who was only three when they came, enjoyed this enormously. Aidan was seven, Pierce almost six, and these two were able to use the admirable books, *Colour-Factor Mathematics* by H. A. Thompson, that came with the set. When I would ask what they wanted to do first in the morning, the answer was always Colour-Factor. We might find ourselves spending whole mornings building up the series of square numbers. Odd and even, prime numbers, area, volume, fractions, Highest Common Factor, Lowest Common Multiple, the use of different bases were all tangible, you could say brilliantly clear.

They did not rush into this all at once; following the instructions of Mr. Thompson, we worked with the blocks for quite a long time referring to them only by colour. It is remarkable how much understanding can be reached in this way. The children's first workbook runs to sixty pages of lucid instructions, questions and diagrams without using a numeral. On the first page there is simply a full-size, full-colour representation of each of the blocks. At the top of the page you read 'Here is a picture of your coloured blocks.' At the bottom, 'Can you find a real block to fit each of the shapes in the picture?'

On the last page of the same book, *Pre-Number Mathematics*, there is a diagram of two rows of blocks with these questions underneath:

$$\text{Is it true that} \quad r - s = l + p?$$
$$\text{and} \quad r - (s + p) = l \,?$$
$$\text{Does} \quad p = r - (l + s)\,?$$
$$\text{and} \quad p = r - l - s\,?$$
$$\text{Is} \quad p + s = r - l\,?$$

After suggesting that the student make some patterns for himself and write them down in ways that are correct, Mr. Thompson says,

'I hope you can now look at a pattern of blocks and see a great deal more than you could at first. You will be surprised how good you will become at this, and it will help you a great deal later on.'

And so it does help a great deal later on. It is not only that when the children start to use number names they can call up a considerable range of combinations about which they are quite certain. The letters just above are juggling with the fact that $2 + 3 + 4 = 9$. The children know this without having to pause or count; they know how the familiar blocks fit together. We used to play a game of taking a random handful of blocks out of a bag and adding the number of units. I remember Pierce glancing at his handful and saying 'The square of six plus one.' And he had indeed got thirty-seven. He was still six when he found out for himself the principle of addition of indices; Alasdar in consequence made for him a little cardboard slide-rule.

Then you could say that there was a useful side-effect, since the clear instructions in workbooks gave them something to read, followed by something to do when they had read it. They learnt to say 'plus' and 'minus' from the beginning, and not to suppose that the minus sign means you must 'take away' something — a cause of much confusion at later stages. I know that other ranges of mathematical material exist but I doubt if anything else could be of such help to children working with an untrained teacher. I know I learnt a good deal myself, and now that Oliver is seventeen, in his second term doing a degree in mathematics at Trinity College, he has told me two or three times, without any prompting, that it is only now he realises how good Colour-Factor were.

# Chapter 9
# ONE BY ONE
# THEY GO TO SCHOOL

BEFORE I write about the children's experiences in school I should define my terms, keeping them as free from complication as I can.

First level or primary schooling in Ireland usually takes children aged four to eleven or twelve. Most schools are 'national schools', paid for by the State but managed by religious managers, either Catholic or Protestant. There are a small number of private primary schools, fee-paying, most often they are the junior section of a secondary school.

Second level or post-primary serves children aged eleven or twelve upward to seventeen or eighteen. Until 1967 the division was between private fee-paying *secondary schools*, partly financed from public funds, almost all organised by religious and teaching academic subjects and *Vocational Schools*, financed by public funds, teaching a mixture of technical and academic subjects.

Since 1967 the distinctions have become blurred. Few schools require fees. The vocational schools and their successors, community schools, offer more academic subjects while the secondary schools try to offer more vocational training. Both schools do the uniform State examinations, the Intermediate Certificate and the Leaving Certificate. The latter increasingly requires that students plan to take a pass paper or an honours paper in each subject. Earlier, two honours permitted university entrance. Now university entrance has become more competitive; it would be difficult to get in with less than three or four. A pass in Irish was and is required for the National University.

Third level includes the universities, colleges of technology, National College of Art, and such like. In Dublin there is a choice of university: Trinity College, an old foundation which is itself a

59

university, and UCD, University College Dublin, a constituent college of National University of Ireland.

It is generally supposed that in Ireland, as in many other countries, parents are legally obliged to send their children to school. Parents in Britain and in the USA have in recent years been discovering that the laws are more flexible than they appeared, but in Ireland parents are fortunate enough to find their rights acknowledged in the Constitution.

Article 42

1. The State acknowledges that the primary and natural educator of the child is the family and guarantees to respect the inalienable right and duty of parents to provide, according to their means, for the religious and moral, intellectual, physical and social education of their children.

2. Parents shall be free to provide this education in their homes or in private schools or in schools recognised or established by the State.

3. 1° The State shall not oblige parents in violation of their conscience and lawful preference to send their children to schools established by the State, or to any particular type of school designated by the State.

   2° The State shall, however, as guardian of the common good, require in view of actual conditions that the children receive a certain minimum education, moral, intellectual and social.

For our family, learning at home began because of our location and continued because it worked and we enjoyed it. There were other reasons also. We found that we were not happy about national schools, partly because of class size and teacher attitude, partly because of the position of the Irish language.

This country gained its independence in 1921. During the following decade the Professor of Education in University College Dublin, Dr T. Corcoran, S.J., insisted that the national language could be restored to common use through the schools. He claimed that children of three could be taught to think in Irish, 'the English thought-ruts not having been sufficiently deepened to prevent the formation of a perfect new system of Irish thought-ruts.'

Teachers were encouraged to pretend that they did not understand English. *The Report of the Commission on Primary Education*, published in 1929, showed that such subjects as art, handwork and rural science had to be pushed out in order to make room in the timetable for Irish. The Montessori method had been creeping into National Schools, but the Reverend Professor took a vehement dislike to it and not only did it wither, but prejudice among teachers trained in his time lasted for many years. (See a series of articles by T. Corcoran, S.J., in *The Irish Monthly* March-July 1924).

Reaction set in, but not soon enough for us. In 1966 Dr John MacNamara published a study of bilingualism in primary education in which he showed that the importance given to Irish was a major factor in depressing performance in IQ tests and in English reading. In 1969 a teachers' study group, reporting on a proposed new curriculum, said:

> . . . there are children leaving National Schools who, in all their time there, have scarcely ever opened a book other than a textbook, or who have never been encouraged to develop their natural interest in living creatures, who have never been asked to listen to a piece of music, and who have never made anything with their hands apart from the plasticine figures which they made when in infants' class.

We decided that our children should at least be able to read and write correctly in one language before learning a difficult second language. It seems now that they would have learnt much better Irish if they had stayed at home for lessons with Sean instead of going to schools where teachers changed frequently and some thoroughly off-putting methods of teaching had evolved, supported in the boys' schools by violent punishment. Ironic, since it was principally on account of the language that we did send them to school. However, it is time to tell how each survived.

## Barbara (February, 1948)

She was born into ice and snow, and too many theories about

open air and breastfeeding, but she grew up very active and competent, able to crawl quite fast at the age of five months. She literally ran before she walked; she could get around so easily on hands and feet that she did not waste time toddling. When she was eighteen months old she had come over to the spring with me for water. She stood up straight, put her hands up over her head, and ran back to the house through the flowers like a little deer. And like a little deer she used to stand beside the purple sprouting broccoli, hands behind her back, nibbling the delicate buds.

Insets, paint and charcoal were familiar before she was as year old. I have indicated that she was not fortunate in her introduction to reading, but she made excellent use of the *Writing Patterns.* She was six when we set off, Barbara, myself and four younger children to stay with my father in Pontevedra in Northern Spain. She was responsible enough to escort Alasdar and Tinu through murderous traffic to a school where I hoped they would pick up some Spanish. They seem to have done more teaching of English than learning of Spanish, but the nuns set Barbara to embroidery and she produced surprisingly good work. Who knows, this may have contributed to later skill in weaving.

Before she was seven she began to teach herself to play the piano, using a strip of card which fits behind the keyboard. By the time she was nine she was able to make a dress for Janet without any help; it was tweed, had a zip and set-in pleats, and she made it all by herself from the pattern instructions. By this time she was at school. When we moved to Dublin we found that if she went to the nearest national school she would have shared one teacher with more than forty children; if she went a little further, to a particularly popular school, she would have been one of a class of eighty.

We had not money for a private primary school, so she continued to learn at home. A year or so later we decided that we could manage to send her to the school run by Religious of Christian Education, where we found that some of the material we liked was in use and the nuns were entirely amiable. Her reading was less than satisfactory but was compensated for by her capacity in art, music and mathematics. She loved her piano teacher and learnt very well with her.

When she was due to move up to secondary school she and Tinu changed for various reasons to the Loreto nuns, nearer home. Here the greatest benefit was during the years she was taught by Sister

Norbert, who had been an artist before she entered and who was able to teach art, religion, history and English so that each supported the other.

For years in both schools she used to be very anxious about her homework; all the time she was working at one subject she would be worrying about whether she would have time for the next. I did what I could with the help of a kitchen timer and reassurance, but I often wondered why, if homework was so important, it was necessary to spend so many hours in class as well. While she was at secondary school she was 'spotted' as a potential swimmer. Training was demanding; she had to go a half-hour journey late in the evening twice a week; competitions with her club were often held in unheated baths. She developed a beautiful smooth breast stroke and won a medal at national level and lost, or at least channelled, some of her anxiety.

It was in the year before she finished school, when she was sixteen, that she had such a run of success with art competitions; first place in both Caltex and Glen Abbey, each bringing an amount of money that was considerable at the time, and also an adult competition that awarded free tuition in lithography. (The photograph on page 2 is of the winning entry, painted when she was sixteen.) When I asked her what she wanted to do after school she said her dream was to study at the Royal College of Art in London, but it was impossible; it required five years of art college beforehand, and entry was extremely restricted.

She sat for a scholarship to the National College of Art in Dublin. There were thirty entrants for six places; she did not get one. Since there had been 30,000 entries for Caltex, we thought this was hardly reasonable; we had a pretty good idea of why it happened. Séan pursued enquiries, tracked down the official responsible. It was as we supposed; her drawing was excellent, it was her Irish that was not good enough. And she had passed in Irish in the Leaving Certificate, set by the same Department that ran the College!

She did, subsequently, try the Art College for a term, was not impressed; went to work as *au pair* with a cousin of mine in New Jersey; in her spare time she worked at the Art Students' League. When the family moved to Washington D.C. she found out that the Corcoran School was the place to go. Here for six months she studied pottery under a strict Japanese master; nine out of ten pots were cut in half to monitor technique; very few were fired. I delight

63

in the collection she brought home. She must have been promising; when she was leaving one of her teachers said he hoped to meet her again when she was famous; she answered that she did not want that, she just wanted to be a good potter.

It was not possible. She could not find the teaching or the facilities she would have needed, so she used her savings to pay for lessons with a Swedish weaver, Lilli Böhlin, who had a studio in Dublin. Here Barbara worked a twelve hour day, turned out a variety of fabrics. By the time her second month was up Lilli said she need not pay any more fees if Lilli might sell her tapestries instead.

The ceramics and the weaving combined to win her a scholarship to Kilkenny Design Workshops. The Finnish Director of the Workshops said he had picked her because he could see that she had not been processed by an art school. He even commissioned a tapestry and hung it in his own house. After a most valuable year as the only student among a group of designers from different countries she fortunately answered an advertisement for a designer of weaving for McNutt's of Carrigart, a Donegal firm producing hand-woven tweed.

Here she was soon asked to take charge of a side-line they had just set up, an experiment in screen-printing designs onto tweed. She had to learn from books about printing and dyeing and then teach local boys. Soon she asked if she might use her own designs. These were well adapted to the rough surface of the tweed; some she printed over herringbone or traditional pepper-and-salt weaves. They sold well; they were remarked at the Interstoff trade fair; friends recognised her prints as far apart as Kansas and Copenhagen.

She was by now nearly twenty-one, old enough to apply to the Royal College of Art. At first they turned her down because she had not got the necessary diploma, but on appeal, backed with curriculum vitae, which showed a good deal more experience than art college could have provided, she was accepted. McNutt's continued to take her designs, which helped with fees. (I am happy to say that their tweeds are now so well known in Paris that they do not need any prints.)

Barbara was awarded her Master's degree, M.Des.R.C.A., at the same time as her future husband, Joe, who had been studying graphics at the College. They shared poverty for a time in Italy, but gradually both began to prosper. She found she could sell designs not only in Europe but even in Japan; she began to lecture in two Colleges of Art. Two years in succession she was invited to exhibit among the 'top twenty' at the Design Centre. Joe, meanwhile, was being asked to do more and more drawings for *The Observer, The Times,* and *Radio Times* and many magazines. He has illustrated a series of books by Frank Muir about a puppy called What-a-Mess. In the most recent of these we can all recognise a new individual among the collection of minor characters that Joe adds to the stories. It is, unmistakeably, Joe and Barbara's two-year-old baby, Sam.

Sam, for his part, has completely changed Barbara's life, at least for the present. He is even more attractive and wakeful than she used to be herself. He lives the life of Riley, some afternoons at an excellent mother-and-baby drop-in centre, others enjoying the shiny floors of the Royal Academy. Recently Barbara has been asked to go back to lecturing a few days each term in Winchester and she has been able to persuade Sam to let her go. Nothing fits in perfectly with baby care, but freelance designing at home is one of the best combinations for the present.

### Alasdar (April, 1949)

Alasdar seems to have been always calm and thoughtful. Looking back, I see him out in the garden, rocking quietly on a very small rocking horse, then bringing over a bucket of tasty stones to feed it, just as he would later look after all the needs of his motorcycle after a run.

I have told how he discovered the function of letters before he was two, progressed to arranging dozens of letter and picture cards, and read his first book when he was three. He has told me that he got great pleasure from a set of plastic gears, which may have set him on the road towards engineering; certainly Meccano can be given credit for guiding him in that direction. He spent one term at Montessori school, but since he had been able to read for some time and preferred to do arithmetic by himself, it seemed he would be better off back at home. Lessons with him were delightful. At the age of six he would sometimes waken his father in the morning to do some geometry. After the move to the Mill House, when we had introduced Mrs. Frankenberg's *Latin with laughter,* he would often pull me upstairs to make some more funny sentences about sailors and islands and wasps.

When he was eight we enrolled him in the junior department of the nearest (fee-paying) boys' school. His classmates found it hard to believe that he had not been to school before, but they did not hold it against him. After all, they shared the same problems. One morning the class counted how often a certain brother used the 'leather'; the count was sixty blows.

I have to admit that he was not depressed. On the contrary, it was only when he was away for a few days that I realised how much we missed the new collection of funny stories he used to bring home to lunch every day. School was deeply boring but he found other things to do. He took up card tricks which developed into magic or conjuring and was allowed to join the adult 'Magic Circle' when he was twelve. He decided to be a pilot, taught himself navigation, used to cycle out to the military airport where he was allowed into training cockpits, encouraged to play his mouth-organ and given dinner in the mess.

Feeling that the boredom in school was needless, I asked if he might bring in useful books to read in class when he had done whatever was required. This was not thought possible, but the headmaster recommended that he be brought to a psychologist to see whether he was too slow or too quick. This turned out to be a very helpful meeting for some of his siblings. The psychologist to whom we were sent, Fr Dermot Casey, S.J., thought schools unreasonable in collecting young children into very large classes while having older, more competent children in smaller groups. He managed to run a special school of his own, with classes of only ten, to give a break to children under pressure. Of Alasdar he said that he was the most intelligent child he had tested — but then it was with other problems that people came to him. Anyway, he was interested in what we were doing at home and adopted *Colour-Factor* and *Writing Patterns* for his school. Later on the school gave both Pierce and Thomas just what suited them.

It was too late to rescue Alasdar, but he did find more scope in the secondary school, with a particularly good geography master. The teaching of Irish was as brutal as ever, but he did well in everything else. His early Latin turned out to have been useful after all .

The day he returned to school after his Intermediate exam —

probable age, fourteen — he came home at lunchtime and said he would commit suicide if he had to go back. It was partly the prospect of having the same master for Irish, but also the recognition that the new mathematics master did not know any maths. We tried to see the headmaster to discuss a year in France, or some other possibility, but he had no time to spare. We turned to the other option, a technical school run by the Vocational Education Committee and got quite a different welcome; a short intelligence test, and he was urged to start the next day. Having a practical workshop class every day as well as the academic subjects made a great difference to him. He was especially fortunate in going to the school just when Anton Trant was teaching there for a couple of years. Mr. Trant has since been engaged in setting up pilot projects in environmental studies in each country of the EEC.

From this school Alasdar got a scholarship to study engineering at a college of Technology. For this course he required the British A Level exams; he got four A levels in one year. While he was studying there his name was entered for the draftsman section of the annual international competition for apprentices. He was adjudged best in Ireland at freehand technical drawing, second best all round. He was doing only a few hours a week while the other competitors were working full time. This skill was not of any special use to him later, but I think it deserves mention as a result of his youthful work with geometrical insets.

During his last years at the College he became depressed. I do not know all the causes; several members of the family are plagued by depression at intervals. I am fairly sure that a contributory cause was the introduction of 'management studies' and a visit to a factory where he saw the sort of repetitive work he would be expected to manage. He had, of course, worked at all sorts of jobs each summer, but he had never been asked to snip bits of wire all day.

When he had completed his engineering studies he was encouraged to do an MSc in Computer Science at Trinity College, studying problems of information retrieval. This led on to a Ph.D. During his time in the Department of Computer Science he was particularly pleased when he enabled his department to score over the Arts faculties. *The Irish Times* runs Literary Competitions, usually humorous. One such competition required a story in the manner of Myles na gCopaleen. It was under this name that Flann

O'Brien used to contribute an erudite and deeply funny column to that paper. Myles, or Flann, was Alasdar's favourite author; to excel in imitating him in his own paper was a triumph, and definitely one up for the Computer Scientists.

Since then he has worked in a consultancy based in Trinity College, spent a couple of years in London on a project to help airlines keep track of goods, and is now back in Dublin again as a subsidiary of a USA software company. He is just unwinding after a full year's work, often up to midnight, putting together a compiler. His 'fairly serious' opinion is that a great many firms, including our own Post Office, have rushed into investment in computers when they might do better with adding machines; the Post Office at least would be able to send us smaller telephone bills.

## Tinu (July, 1950)

While Alasdar still holds that neither he nor his brothers and sisters should have been sent to school, Tinu is content to say how glad she is to have escaped several years of boredom. She was always a whirlwind. When she arrived at the Mill House, aged four, with a couple of terms of formal Montessori behind her, she could get through a useful morning's work in a very short time and play for the rest of the day in the wilderness at the end of the garden. I can still see myself and the four-year-old Tinu sitting on the sunny, uncarpeted stairs with the story of 'Lambkin and the Drumkin' when she had come begging 'listen to me reading'.

Tinu used to do a great deal of painting on the kitchen wall, drawing on the marble table. She was the first to break into the child Art competitions, the first to decide that she had had enough of them. She continued to draw flowers and Sean's Birthday Book has a flower for every year, as well as her beautifully written contributions.

She went to the same two schools as Barbara. They both made good friends, both were constantly in trouble for chattering and scribbling during class, both did well academically in every subject except Irish. Indeed, one year each got the class medal for Religious Knowledge. Like Barbara, Tinu used to work so hard for exams that I thought a parent's most useful role was to keep down the pressure. She got her Leaving Certificate at sixteen with four honours; if she had waited until the following year this would have won her a university scholarship.

Her application to study in the Botanic Gardens was unsuccessful, so she did a course in dress designing; she had been making her own dresses for years, but often wanted to make changes in the pattern. It is possible that her early work with geometric insets helped her not only with school geometry, which she loved, but also with the pattern making in this course; she certainly completed it rapidly. She worked both with a couture house and with a smaller manufacturer, but the tension at the first, the economic constraints of the second, decided her to find a different career.

She was now eighteen, and applied again to the Botanic Gardens to work for a diploma in amenity horticulture. A friend of hers applied at the same time, they were both accepted, and during the course they got married, the first pair of students to do so. This course, half work in the open air, half study (with a nine mile bicycle ride to get to it) suited her very well; at the end she won the gold medal for the year and she and her husband both had the option of taking up university scholarships.

The ease with which she learned about plants may relate to a favourite game that I did not mention in the first section. If there were four children playing, they would cover their eyes, I would go around the garden selecting leaves, four of each kind, distribute a similar bunch to each child and see who would be first to find where they had come from. Then we would talk about them, glossy ivy, spotted lungwort, striped lamium, whorled woodruff, and so on.

Sadly, the young couple found that marriage and a baby did not make it easy for both to continue their careers. They parted unhappily when their little boy was two but now scars have healed and Ivan, who now lives in London with his mother, is able to come over to Ireland for camping holidays with his father and surprise him with his knowledge of plants. The advantage of a qualification in horticulture was that Tinu was able to find a series of jobs with a house provided; a particularly pleasant one in Surrey. She could have Ivan with her as well, and even managed to help him learn the way she had done herself; when he went to school at five they said he had a reading age of nine. Years of work in Britain allowed her to qualify for a grant to study and she is now completing her second year of very hard work for the Institute of Landscape Architects.

Before I leave Tinu I feel I must copy a page she wrote in the Birthday Book when she was eleven. Not only does it let her speak for herself, but it gives a less rose-coloured picture of family life than I may have painted. Even while I pass it on I must insist that it is describing a holiday away from home and soothing 'lessons'.

*Breakfast with Thomas*

Everyone is sitting down, when He appears in the doorway. His first words are, 'Mama, where my place?' 'Here on the bench' is Mama's reply. 'I don't want to sit beside Pierce' whines Thomas. 'You will have to' says Jenny. 'I won't' is Thomas' answer. 'Oh, shut up Thomas' or 'Be quiet Thomas and sit there' is hurled upon him from every side. Soon Thomas sits down when sitting he smacks Pierce. Pierce smacks Thomas and soon both are bawling their heads off. Soon Pierce stops, but Thomas goes on for a long time. At long last he stops when put in a different place not beside Pierce but soon his whine changes to 'Mama I want coppee' He is given his 'coppee' and is quite, but not for long soon it is 'Mama I want more sugar on mine porridge' He is given sugar and when it melts he cannot see it so asks for 'More sugar' This goes on until his porridge is taken (usually) It is often Barbara who says 'Thomas I will put you out' and often me who starts to copie him whining. 'Stop Tinu' says Thomas. 'No.' 'Stop Tinu' 'Not unless you stop whining' This kind of row goes on until Mama or Dada shouts 'Tinu stop teasing. Thomas stop whining'
But I am glad to say breakfast is soon over and everyone is glad even though Thomas goes on whining, whining, whining . . . . . .
Tinu, Age 11.

If I had not her word for it I would hardly believe that Thomas had ever been like that. Of course he was still very small, and he had not yet found his fulfilment in birds.

### Janet (March, 1952)

Fortunately a day in the life of a five-and-a-half year old Janet has also been preserved. Not an average day, or I would not have been prompted to borrow her pencil and write it down while it was happening, but still a very good indication of her life-style.

It was a Sunday, but she turned up in the morning with her workbook in her hand and asked to have her pencil sharpened. It was one of the Ridout *English Workbooks,* with blanks requiring to be filled in with the correct words from a list provided as, 'Bottles are made of ———'. A different sort of problem on each page. She had already done easier workbooks writing in mixture of capitals and cursive. I thought this book was grown-up enough to need proper cursive handwriting. Nevertheless she had done three pages by lunchtime. As soon as lunch was finished she was back on the job. By the time she had done seven pages the writing was coming quite easily but I felt the questions were getting rather difficult. I persuaded her to do some easier word-building for a rest. Then Sean offered to take the six elders for a walk, leaving me at home with the baby. Janet was quite willing to go. 'Yes,' she said, 'And I'll come back happy and ready to do some more work.'

It was while she was out that I took her pencil and noted down what I have just written. When she came back she did two more pages while I was getting dinner ready, making a total of nine pages between eleven in the morning and half-past-six. Several times I asked, 'Don't you think you've done enough, Jenny?' The answer would be, 'I like it.'

That was fine, but the other half was just as important. After dinner she volunteered to do the washing-up along with the older children and then insisted on doing a clean-up of the gas cooker, which meant taking out and washing the bars on the top, the tray underneath. And *then* she washed the large kitchen floor.

Bursts of energy like that did not happen every day; though she did spend the whole of Monday filling in more of her workbook I have not recorded any more housework.

She not only drew and painted constantly but liked to work with wood. One of her Caltex prizes was for a model of an Indian village. As well as art prizes (top in Glen Abbey, like Barbara) she used to make a good thing out of her handwriting. School life was like her sisters' until her Intermediate exam. She changed schools after that in order to do honours mathematics, which she would need for architecture. Instead she found herself with a gifted teacher of languages, went to Italy on a working holiday in order to improve her Italian. She also ate pasta, put on just a few pounds of extra weight, and went on a diet when she came home.

We did not recognise what was happening, but before long she was a classic case of *anorexia nervosa*. While she was sitting her Leaving Certificate exam she was living on one apple and a biscuit per day. A variety of causes are suggested for this disease; in Janet's case I think it may have been as simple as the application of will power to slimming. The mysterious thing about anorexia, which is a mental illness that captures more and more school-age girls, is that the victims cannot see themselves; when their bodies are hardly more than skeletons they still think they are fat. Eventually she became a patient in a mental hospital for a few weeks, appeared to recover, decided to train as a psychiatric nurse, did well, but had not really got free from anorexia, was recommended a complete change.

She went to Italy as an *au pair*, to mind a couple of small children. She must have been nineteen. I hope Dr Montessori, in heaven, was pleased with her when she talked herself out of a job, telling the *signora* in a long discussion that it was very bad for the children to have a new person caring for them every six months and that she ought to look after them herself. The *signora* said she had never done any work in her life but she would give it a try, provided 'Gianna' would come back if it got too much for herself.

Janet found herself a job doing macrobiotic cooking in a beautiful house in Fiesole, above Florence. This left her plenty of time to attend classes in the Academy of Fine Arts, from which she graduated four years later with top marks in graphics. She has lived in Florence ever since and has no intention of living anywhere else. She has the tenancy of part of a lovely old convent in the hills above the city; she has managed to keep going by doing all sorts of odd jobs of which the oddest was that of being the only girl caddie on the golf course.

One amusing side of that job was that the players naturally did not suspect that she understood English; another was the humour of the small team of caddies. She has pruned vines, taught English, run a bar in Ustica, and now makes a living by restoring and selling old furniture. All the time she has continued to take lessons in carving whenever she could afford to. In her last letter, after writing of her annual return of enthusiasm for her garden, she says,

'. . . and I want to boast. The teacher is giving me work to do at home — paid — and he asked me to give him a hand working on the most lovely fine carvings in Palazzo Medici Riccardi. You can imagine how flattered I was. Carving may seem simple, but it isn't, not when you are trying to copy Renaissance expertise, with a fluid hand . . .'

## Máire Claire (August, 1953)

Claire was the baby who came to Spain still in her cradle and celebrated her first birthday there on the feast of La Pelegrina, the Patroness of Pontevedra, on August 15th. She was still the baby when we moved to the Mill House and she was therefore the victim of the change to orthodox methods of teaching reading.

As soon as she could walk she made it clear that animals were more deserving of attention than anything else. If we met a horse drawing a cart we had to stand and gaze, no matter how slowly he moved. Over the years she collected mice, a rabbit, a tortoise, puppies, and suffered through some inevitable deaths.

We planned to send her to school when she was eight, but asked whether the nuns thought she should go for a few weeks of the previous term to get used to being in a class. 'No need,' they said, 'if she's anything like her sisters.' Indeed, she did quite well for several years, often meeting work that she had done long before at home.

Fate struck when she was twelve. A school friend was asked to exercise two ponies, brother and sister, Destra and Fay Belle. The latter took Claire's whole attention; when, after a year or so, word came that the ponies were going to be 'put down' unless someone would buy them, there was only one possible solution. Fortunately, uncle's legacy had arrived just in time.

Both girls promised their families that the care of the ponies would not do any harm to their school work, that they would try much harder. A likely story. It turned out that they were missing days, even weeks, of school while searching for grazing for their charges. We had to accept the fact that for Máire Claire it was horses or nothing. Sean and I felt very timid when we went to see the show-jumper and horse breeder Iris Kellett to ask if our daughter might be taken on as a working pupil; we have no connections in the world of Irish horses. We need not have worried; as soon as Fay Belle's name was mentioned, Claire was safely in; it seemed that Ms Kellett had at one time known her quite well.

Claire was able to repay her debt to Fay Belle when she found an Arab sire for a beautiful foal, Fay Belle's first, which gave her a whole new life at the age of nineteen. Claire moved on to a small riding school where she had a lot of responsibility, then, when that closed, she moved again, this time to Burton Hall, where she had the agreeable surprise of being told on her first day that there were pupils waiting for her — they had followed her from the other school.

I, too, had an agreeable surprise at that time. At a Montessori Society meeting I met a young American woman. We found we lived near each other, so we met quite often, with plenty of other interests in common. She was taking riding lessons at Burton Hall; it was only after quite a while that she thought of telling me that there was one particularly encouraging young instructor there; she told you when you did things well instead of nagging when you made mistakes. The others called her Claire. Could she be my Montessori daughter? (Remember that Montessori did not approve of calling attention to mistakes).

Máire Claire took her British Horse Society examination for the Certificate of Horsemastership the summer she was eighteen, the same summer, as it happened, that Barbara was conferred with her M.Des. and Alasdar with his M.Sc. But Burton Hall gave her much more than a certificate. It was a wonderfully rich environment, with people of character and horses of character all working together in a beautiful setting on the slopes of the Dublin mountains. She used to have so many improbable stories to tell us every time she came home that I used to beg her to write it all down.

Qualified, she moved on to a couple of other jobs in Ireland; in one she had a handsome house and stabling for Fay Belle and two foals. Indeed, it was interesting to find how many openings there are in Europe and further afield, for girls skilled with horses. However, she had always had a great many human as well as animal friends; she married Morgan when she was twenty-two; they now have three children, Michael, Hanna and Katy, and live in a little house in the woods in County Wicklow. We are constantly in touch, and she tells me 'lessons' in the mornings are going fine, especially Colour-Factor.

## Aidan (May, 1955)

Aidan appears to have missed the lucky breaks that most of the others have found at some stage but he seems pretty happy in his present life, and has reason to be.

He was a happy small boy, too. Being right in the middle of the family he was bound to miss some attention, but perhaps he had enough older brothers and sisters to make up for that. As far as 'lessons' went, he was unlucky in his introduction to reading, lucky in being the first to meet Colour-Factor maths, but for too short a time before school. He used to get especially good value out of Schools Radio, would be ready with equipment for each science programme, enjoyed the history lesson so much that when he was at school he used to take every Tuesday afternoon off in order to listen. Is it not remarkable that by the time he was twelve he could say that he hated history?

Observation of Aidan's experience at school made me aware as I had not been before of the worthlessness of the average school. He was able to read when he started school at seven; some time later he mentioned that the brother had been getting them to read a page of their horrible little 'reader' from the bottom to the top, to make sure they knew the words. Even while Pierce at home was exploring prime numbers, squares and cubes, area and volume, fractions and decimals, Aidan was burdened with longer and longer 'sums' in pounds, shillings and pence.

Secondary school was as dull as primary, or worse. He was twelve when, with three of the others, he was professionally tested with the WISC intelligence test. He was said to be 'intellectually superior, co-operative and enthusiastic'. His schoolmasters never noticed this, and there was no contact with parents. (I had in the early days made an appointment with the brother who was teaching him in order to show the merits of Colour-Factor; I soon felt that I ought to have stayed in purdah).

Aidan went on to the same technical school as Alasdar but by that time there were changes in staff and atmosphere. It was better than the secondary school, and he did get O Level English and Physics, but when he was due to sit the next set of exams he refused to do so.

After school he and Morgan, Claire's husband, found jobs in a clean, well-run factory near at hand. The money was good, but they were both miserable. They set up a sort of partnership doing odd jobs, painting, gardening and so on. Much of their satisfaction came from a group in which Aidan played the guitar, Morgan piano.

Morgan found his way back into journalism, for which he had trained; Aidan continues to be his own master, living in one of the most beautiful parts of County Wicklow with a wife and two children to match. Helen and the children are not only beautiful but calm, resourceful, confident. Everyone loves to visit them. Whatever about Aidan's schooldays, he is one of the lucky ones now. And the two children, Jasper and Martha, are learning at home as a matter of course.

## Pierce (January, 1957)

Pierce had the air of knowing just what he was looking at as soon as he was born. He grew into a thin, brown, active baby, constantly running away. Neighbours were very good about bringing him back. Barbara put up a notice, 'Please keep gate closed. Wild Babies at large.'

As he grew a little older he took to all the lessons like a duck to water. I had time to realise that Aidan and Claire were not doing so well in reading and brought back the early capitals, with instant success. I have mentioned the time when he was five and asked me, 'Which difficult words?' At six he could read and use the Colour-Factor text books with ease, and work without the book or blocks as well. I noted how one day I came in to the room where he was, found him lying on his back on the floor, and said, 'Hello, I thought you were doing Colour-Factor?'

'I am,' he replied, 'I'm doing twelve eights. Ten eights is eighty, two eights is sixteen, that's ninety-six.'

When I brought him to Aidan's school to enrol they gave him a little test and said that he could cope with third class; when I said second class would do they said that, of course, he would have to start with first class. To read up from the bottom of the page, no doubt.

Fr. Casey, who had tested Alasdar, came to the rescue and took Pierce into his small school, where he spent four fruitful terms, using familiar material, with only ten in his class. By the time he had to leave we had found the German School in Dublin, St.

Kilian's, a co-educational school which was a limited company, owned partly by the parents, partly by the Bonn government.

Here he learnt very happily until he was twelve. Of course he found it difficult to cope with German for half the classes during his first term, but he had time to spare. Good communication with parents was a special feature of the school; so were swimming, art, athletics. And, so different from the experience of Alasdar and Aidan, Pierce never set eyes on a 'leather'. As one of the German teachers said, 'We don't bring the children to school to punish them.' I should add that a fair number of the staff were Irish; the school seemed to attract the best sort of Irish teacher.

By the time he had to go on to secondary school (St. Kilian's being primary only) he was not only good at swimming and athletics and maths, he was happy to be learning four languages: German, Irish, French and English. He had stuck to a voluntary French class when almost all the others had dropped out. In contrast on his second day at the good Irish secondary school he and two other boys were beaten with the leather because they did not know the Irish for whistle. An amazing way of encouraging love of the language.

It was just before the change of schools that we had the batch of IQ tests in the Department of Psychology UCD. I am quite well aware of the limitations of these tests, but when Pierce's report read, 'A bright alert boy, he was highly co-operative in the testing situation and showed intensive interest in the procedure . . . constant effort to solve all the problems . . . powers of observation were particularly evident . . . S. obtained a WISC Full Scale IQ of 137, indicating intellectual function at a "Very superior" level', yet for the next five years in school he never moved much away from mid-level or lower marks in any of his reports, it is hard to believe that the failure was entirely on his side. When, after he had been there a couple of years, a meeting was arranged for parents, we had a short conversation with the priest who had him for Religious Knowledge. 'In my class,' he told us, 'no boy may speak without my permission, and no boy may move without my permission.'

It may be asked why we did not look for a different school. One answer is that as far as we could tell all available boys' schools were much the same, this one better than some others. We were, like so many other parents, hypnotised by the need for the Leaving Certificate.

He did pass this examination with adequate marks, went for a year to a College of Technology, dropped out, spent another year in Europe, partly with Janet in Italy, partly with friends in Crete, where they supported themselves by working at the grape harvest. Worked well, too; he was asked to return, paid more than had been agreed. The depressing effects of school wore off, he came back and did what he should have done at fifteen — went to Atlantic College, Dublin, to study radio and electronics.

This is a private college, with no government grants, charging moderate fees, taking examinations set up by professional bodies. It does not require students to show that they have taken any State examinations; if you are able to follow the course you stay; it is up to yourself. It seems to me that if there were many more such practical establishments large amounts of time and money might be saved. It solved Pierce's problems anyway; he got a job soon after he finished — the head of the college is very helpful — and now he is doing some evening courses to add to his qualifications.

## Thomas (July, 1958)

As a baby, Thomas had one outstandingly good habit; unlike all his brothers and sisters, he used to sleep all night. As he grew a little older, he drew and painted like the others, learnt letters, filled insets but spent much less time at these activities than the others did. He was always out in the garden. I would find him with his little chair arranged so that he could gaze at some bird in the creeper covering the wall. He did not bother to read until he was five, when he brought me a model he had made of a bird on a nest. I admired it, then wrote on a card, NEST, BIRD, WING, TWIG. As soon as he realised there were books about birds he very quickly learnt to read. His contribution to the Birthday Book when he was seven reads:

'I found a hedgesparrow's nest. The first day I found it there were no eggs in it and the next day I looked in it and there was one egg in it and it was blue. And now there are four eggs in it. And it is a very neat nest made of feathers and moss. Then I found a blackbird's nest and I often see him on his eggs and they are big eggs.'

Each year the Birthday Book has more information, more and

better drawings of birds. I must thank a member of the Montessori Society for telling me that the Irish Wildbird Conservancy had room for young members, and for letting me know when one of their annual week-end gatherings would take place. He was ten or eleven at the time; I felt he was a little young to go alone so I went with him. It was marvellous to come across so many adults willing to treat a child as one of themselves. During the Gala Dinner he forgot to eat, he was so excited being able to listen to people who knew so much.

His schooldays sailed by without problems. He went first to Fr Casey's little school, then to the German school and then to an excellent vocational school that allowed him to lead his own life. If he wanted to take a month off during term to act as warden in Cape Clear Observatory, that was fine; his headmaster recognised that this was part of his education.

We tried to make him take school seriously because we mistakenly supposed that if he wanted to have birds as his principal interest he would need some appropriate degree. He very politely ignored our fussing. He had been on the Dublin Committee of the IWC since he was sixteen. He may have had a drawing accepted by *British Birds* before he left school; he has certainly had quite a few since then; that journal even reproduced several pages of his field notes in facsimile. He knew what he was about.

When he left school we found a short course in advertising which paid pocket money to students. He was advised to bring his portfolio to a new partnership which was specialising in graphics, working on commissions from ordinary advertising agencies. He was taken on at once. The firm has grown. It suits Thomas perfectly. He will work overtime for the firm if needed but he can take extra holidays without pay when anything interesting is flying past. He spends every week-end at a different site.

He is one of the committee of three who verify reports of rare birds; a few months ago he was Irish delegate to Israel for a conference on that subject. He has had offers from major publishers asking for drawings and he simply does not have time to take them up; he is too busy observing, corresponding, writing elegant and exact reports. A satisfying life. I remarked to him recently that it would have been much the same if he had never gone to school. He said that was not quite so; he had learnt some chemistry.

## Rebecca (April, 1960)

Rebecca's pre-school years are very much better documented than anyone else's. From shortly before her sixth birthday until she went to school at eight she wrote a sort of journal which gives all sorts of side lights on family life. During most of this time the whole eleven were living at home and the succession of birthdays and other celebrations like first Holy Communion is overwhelming. I had forgotten until I read through these books how much the children mixed with other families. Two sets of Rebecca's own friends turn up constantly. 'We dressed up as witches and Colm was an indian and we made it all dark and told Eoin to come in and then we put him in the pot and cooked him we made stew out of him and ate him up for Dinner and put his funeral up on the top of the page'. That funeral must remain for ever a mystery. Once she goes to school these outside contacts seem to be fewer.

Another interest in these journals is to observe how she changed within six months from a continuous stream of words like that example over to well placed full stops and capitals. By the time she is seven and a half her writing is really elegant. I would not have dreamt of correcting the journal; she learnt about punctuation from her Workbooks, about writing from her *Writing Patterns*.

She had been painting since she was very young. She was three when the Colour-Factor set arrived and for at least the whole of the next year she played with it every single day, often for more than an hour. I was naturally pleased to see such concentration and was often delighted by the complicated pattern she made for herself but

I hesitated to make any reference to number in connection with the blocks. After all Piaget would not expect her to be capable of operational thinking for another three years . . . Once, when I was stepping over the little body on the floor, I noticed that she had placed a pink 2-unit beside a mauve 12-unit and I asked her how many more would she need to make up the whole length. 'Five, of course,' she answered. I am sorry now that I did not take her up on it and see how much interest she had in the mathematical message of her blocks.

But probably it would not have made much difference if I had. She is a puzzle. Not only did she produce far more and far more vivid writing than anyone else of her age, her drawings were also individual, rich in pattern, full of life. She read a great deal; a few days after her seventh birthday the journal tells the whole story of one of Laura Ingalls Wilder's books, *The Long Winter,* and Rebecca compares it with several other books about the same family. She climbed up the rope on the tree the day we first hung it up. When she was at the German school she found that she was the fastest girl runner. She can swim, and when Claire was working in Burton Hall Rebecca had the opportunity to spend all her free time there working and riding and Claire said she was very good; she was certainly very happy, and lost her heart to one of the ponies.

When she joined Pierce and Thomas at St. Kilian's it was decided that she did not need to attend any of the English classes so she spent her time sharing German classes with both first class and second class. She stayed there contentedly until she had to change to secondary school. She went to a convent school run by Dominican nuns. Classes were streamed and she was placed in the A stream so that she could continue German. The benevolent sister encouraged the new class to sit with their friends. Rebecca naturally found herself between strangers, since nobody else from her old school had moved with her, but the unfortunate nuns spent a good deal of energy during the next five years trying to prise apart the trio that formed on that first day.

Though she was so often in some kind of trouble along with the other two none of it was serious. She thoroughly adopted the prevailing outlook. I do not at all blame the school, which was very good, but the whole system. As the exam seasons approached she would bury herself in study, constantly issuing warnings, 'You know I'm going to fail my Inter.' 'You know I'm going to fail my

Leaving.' I remember one of our many rows when she had asked for some help with French and I read a sentence with an approximation to a French accent. My position was that I would not mind if she failed provided she liked French. She stated *her* position, which summarised so much. 'I don't want to know French, I just want to get my Leaving.' (Incidentally, there are no oral exams in modern languages at school level).

Well, she worked hard, got her precious Leaving with four honours, an A in history. She had not only absorbed what she was told but could hand it back lucidly expressed in pleasing handwriting. But that was four years ago and she has not shown a sign since of interest in history or economics or languages or any of those things she worked at and she seems for the time at least to have battened down the creativity with which she was as gifted as any of her sisters.

She was, of course, qualified to go on to university but she was determined on no account to be a 'student'. She did part of a secretarial course, then got through the stiff competition to work for Aer Lingus — and found herself doing totally boring work that would have suited a twelve year old. Of course working for an airline carries the bonus of cheap flights; she has been able to visit Barbara and Tinu in London, Janet in Italy, but is it worth it? She was offered a job elsewhere, but was persuaded to stay by promise of something more interesting to do. Now there is a rumour that all the complicated clerical work she is doing will be, at enormous expense, automated. She exemplifies the fate of thousands, even millions, in our society. I believe she might be lucky to lose her job and find out what she could really do.


**Eoin (November, 1962)**

One of my favourite memories of Eoin as a small boy belongs to a day when he and Oliver were about to move into a different bedroom. We were going to paint it first. He is alone, standing up on a bench, scraping old paint from the wall. I hear him say to himself, 'At the age of five I am a very helpful boy . . . I am honest, too.' The honesty had shown itself the day before, when he found a threepenny bit and had given it to me.

It was true that he was always helpful and interested; he would see what needed to be done instead of asking what you wanted — or dodging. In the first part of the book I have told about his deafness and how he was consequently late in speaking, and how he so remarkably read his first four words. I suppose this held him back just enough to make it possible for himself and Oliver to do lessons together. We had a very good time with word games and geography. Cooking together gave us enlightening experience of multiplication, division, fractions and so on, as well as time to talk about why we need food. Eoin's independence in cooking his grandmother's birthday cake when he was six is also part of the early record.

I heard a Professor of Psychology say that children with an IQ of less than 120 should not be forced to learn a second language; this lecture was the first threat to the tyranny of Irish in schools. For me it raised the question of whether it would be fair to Eoin to send him to a school where he would have to work through a second language as well as learning a third.

I found that he could be tested at a Child Guidance Centre so I brought himself and Oliver along. I was even allowed to sit in the background since Eoin was a bit anxious. (Oliver went off without a second thought). It was agreeable to see how eagerly he arranged blocks and copied shapes as he was directed. One outcome was that the two little boys were found to be well up to requirements; the director of the centre said it was as pity more parents did not do the sort of thing we had done. The other was that we were encouraged to get a more thorough check and it was discovered that Eoin was, as we had suspected, slightly deaf. A small operation was arranged.

Eoin and Oliver not only had the advantages of St. Kilian's as a primary school — small classes, shorter hours, specialist teachers, very good contact between teachers and parents — they were able to stay there right up to the top. After years of debate the school had become a secondary school as well. The children were able to stay with their friends, with teachers they knew. At the same time there was sufficient variety because most of the German teachers came on three year contracts. Of course the boys found some reasons to grumble but whenever they heard about their brothers' schools they acknowledged how fortunate they were. Their confidence was built up, not cut down. We were fortunate also, since fees were very low.

It is a general complaint that, though pressure for examination results was bad enough fifteen years ago, when the elders of our family were facing their 'Leaving', it has now become very much greater. It was heartening to see how rationally Eoin made his plans. He had pretty well made up his mind to train as a chef, but it seemed prudent to qualify for Trinity College. He picked his five preferred subjects and ignored the rest, worked just as hard as he judged would get him through, but not a minute more.

All went well. He was offered a place to read geography in Trinity. Meanwhile, he had been going around fixing interviews to get himself selected for the chef training course. He worked as a caterer on his own during the summer, cooking for a recording studio. He is now almost at the end of the two year training course. For his practical work he was fortunate enough to place himself with a really top Swiss chef, Josef Frei, who owns Killakee House, not far from home. Josef now invites him to come and work for him at week-ends and any time he can, which should be very helpful if the next stage of Eoin's plans come off. He finds that a degree course in Human Nutrition has been organised between one of the Colleges of Technology and Trinity College. This interests him very much; chemistry and geography were his best subjects; it has become a matter of urgency for all of us to find out how this small planet can best nourish its owners. I do hope Eoin will be accepted.


## Oliver (July, 1964)

Oliver was 'reading for meaning' before he was two. If I said 'Time for bed' before he wanted to go he would sometimes fetch his card saying 'BED' and throw it away to demonstrate his disagreement. He and Eoin slept, or were supposed to sleep, in a pair of small bunk beds. It used to seem impossible to subdue them at night time. But sometime while Oliver was still quite small I chanced on an effortless remedy. I had only to begin a story about how Oliver was out in the garden and his friend Ant crawled up a blade of grass and found Oliver . . . Then I would ask him what happened next, anything might; Ant not only had a van in which to travel, but another friend, Ghost . . .

Imagination filled part of his day. He pretended to be other people almost as soon as he could talk. When he was rather older I watched him being both a cowboy and an Indian having a fight,

jumping round to face his other self. Another part of his personality was fascinated by matching such things as the covers of books with the illustrations inside, and noting the smallest discrepancies.

Early lessons were pure fun. True, as I have said, he went on strike in the matter of reading when he was three. but he had already grasped the essentials. I find this paragraph ending a book review that I wrote at the time, (of Engleman's *Give Your Child a Superior Mind*):

Three-year-old beside me has just shown me a letter he has drawn. 'You put it in the middle of Barbara's letter and you put S beside it and you have BUS.' Then he wrote BUS. Next he showed me a drawing he had just made of a man with his mouth wide open and asked me to tell him to close it. When the man did not obey he suggested that I whisper in his ear. It seems to me that that's what most children are like and you'd have to squash them a lot to fit them into the logical pattern of the *'Superior Mind'*.

Reading returned; when he was seven I found seven books under his pillow.

In the chapter about painting I have written about the lovely things he made before he was two and a half, and about how he gave it up before I recognised what was happening. The fortunate outcome is that during the last three years he has become fascinated by European painting. He haunts the National Gallery, reads and copies. He celebrated the end of school by a holiday last summer partly in Paris, partly in London, his time spent mostly in the great galleries.

St. Kilian's wanted him to learn some German before he started in the primary school. For a term he went to kindergarten three mornings a week, had lessons at home the other mornings. To real school he went every day. When holidays came, he announced, 'We're going to do lessons every morning. First we'll do Colour-Factor, then workbook, then we'll read my *American Indian Mythologies*.' He said the same thing next holidays, but somehow brothers and sisters and friends all on holidays were very distracting. I have never found it satisfactory to do our kind of lessons while people are attending school. School takes the edge off their energy. Better to play chess instead.

I think a sample report puts both Oliver and St. Kilian's in a good light. This was when he was eleven.

> Oliver is an intelligent, hard-working pupil. He has an enquiring mind and is tolerant of views different from his own. He participates well in class activities, and in discussion makes his point clearly and logically. Academically he has attained a good standard, particularly in French, for which he has a natural flair. Very satisfactory pupil.

In the following years he came to use the school more as a resource. For example, he greatly appreciated a German art master, and stayed in on half-days for lessons with him. On the other hand, he was not happy with physics class, so ignored it and enrolled himself in evening classes at the Pre-University Centre. His special good fortune was to have good maths teaching right up the school and especially from an enthusiastic young maths specialist, Mr. David Howard, in the last two years. He took his Leaving Certificate when he was sixteen and now, at seventeen, seems to be comfortable working for a mathematics degree in Trinity College. It is hard work, but he finds time for friends and reading and art. So far, so fortunate.

This family record requires to be filled out with comment on three matters of general importance, religion, intelligence and health.

## Religion

Occasional reference to someone's First Holy Communion do not give a true picture. Sean and I were brought together because we were both 'Sheed & Ward Catholics'. I refer to the life-enhancing publishing house set up by Frank Sheed and Maisie Ward. We enjoyed reading theology, we enjoyed the liturgy. Naturally, this permeated family life. Very much so, since the family would not have been anything like the size it is but for Catholic teaching.

One reason we kept them out of school was that we did not like the idea of assembly-line First Communion class. At least half of bed-time reading was religious. (Helen Wadell's *Stories from Holy Writ* are beautiful. A Sheed & Ward publication, *St. Patrick's Summer* by Marigold Hunt, was read over and over again). Why has it not worked out, why has it not produced at least half-a-dozen regular Sunday Mass-attending Catholics? There are a few; it would not be proper to say which is which, but I daresay it is easy to guess that the boys who attended leathering schools are the most disaffected. As for the rest, one of the girls said when I asked her, that celebrations at home were much more fun than anything at the church. It is a large question; if I had dwelt on it, it would have swamped the rest of the book.

## Health

Not without importance. It could be luck, it could be their grandmother's prayers, but though some or all of the children have climbed ropes and trees, walked on walls, swam, ridden horses and motorbikes, they have remained uninjured — even at a time when collar-bones and pelvises were being cracked wholesale among their friends in the neighbourhood.

I suspect that the independence and control over movement

fostered by Montessori should have some of the credit. *The Self Respecting Child*, by Alison Stallibrass, discusses the need to let children find out how to control their bodies. She also describes the 'Peckham Experiment' where the activities of children mingled with those of adults. It seems to me that Thomas, birdwatching regardless of age, Claire and Rebecca riding with young and old, were similarly fortunate.

Negative records are not reliable, but in all of Rebecca's journal there is no mention of anyone except Mama being sick. I understand from friends that colds regularly do the rounds of playgroups and infant schools; I believe that ours avoided a good deal of infection. At any rate, apart from the intervention to cure Eoin's deafness, and the removal of a set of tonsils and adenoids, they quite avoided hospital. Come to think of it, using neither National Schools nor much of the Health Service, the family has not been much of a burden on the State.


**Intelligence and IQ Tests**

There is much debate about the value of intelligence tests. Obviously, they must ignore vast areas of human competence. But it is claimed that the standard tests measure ability to engage in the activities for which schools are organised. For that reason I think our record is significant. There is available a record on a very much larger scale with which it can be compared.

All 8,000 children born in England during one week of March 1946 were entered in a survey. They have been interviewed and assessed at intervals ever since. A huge amount of material has been collected and many different investigations have been based on it. I quote here from one of these, *The Home and The School*, by Dr J. W. B. Douglas (Panther 1967).

Clever children are of course found in large families as well as in small, but the average level of measured ability declines with each increase in family size . . . It is desirable to see whether the relationship between family size and mental ability which has been shown in other studies holds in this one too. The answer is that it does. The test scores of these eleven-year-olds decline as families get larger, so that children with five brothers and sisters make scores that are on average 6.9 points of T score below those of only children. As each child is added to the family, so the average score drops by a little more than that observed in the Scottish Mental Survey . . . Children from really large families (of six or more) are at as much of a disadvantage if their fathers are in the professions as if they follow some middle-class occupation. pp.122-125.

Well, there you are. It was around the age of eleven or twelve that several of our set were tested. It may be remembered that Eoin's deafness had made him appear a bit slow and that I brought the two youngest for tests. The results were sufficiently interesting to make me curious about the others. These were tested in a university department and we were given quite detailed reports, also a summary which I reproduce here without names.

| WISC Full Scale IQ | Verbal IQ | Performance IQ |
|---|---|---|
| 137 | 131 | 136 |
| 117 | 123 | 108 |
| 122 | 134 | 104 |
| 125 | 128 | 118 |
| 122 | 123 | 118 |

The two youngest were said to be 'Superior'. No figures. Since they were only about four and six years old figures would not count for much anyway, but I have included a school report of Oliver's when he was eleven. Evidence, I think, that even in this 'really large family' the younger children were not at a disadvantage. If not, why not? The Harvard Pre-School Study concluded that the key to later development was probably the attitude of the 'caretaker' while the baby was aged between ten months and eighteen months. Yes, indeed, but I am sure that among the 8,000 March babies there were thousands who had 'caretakers' as responsive as I could have been.

A closer match for our experience comes from Professor Jerome Bruner's five-year Oxford Pre-School Research Project. Here in Dublin last summer he told OMEP (Organisation Mondiale pour l'Éducation Préscolaire) his criterion for good child care: the style of care that *increases the child's capacity to manage its own attention.*

This is an elegant definition of Montessori's purpose. The elements that the Research Project found best for this purpose were, first, activities which have a goal, which give the child feedback, so that she knows what she is doing; it was found also that when the children were encouraged to do something that really stretched their minds they tended to go off on their own to do something of the same order.

I claim simply that activities of this sort are more easily arranged in a home that has a bit of space and access to a garden than in a group, especially if you bear in mind Professor J. McVicar Hunt's basic rule, *The child must always be free to take it or leave it alone.* One implication is that funds should go to housing before they go to schooling; another, simply, *'Anything school can do, you can do better.'*

# Chapter 10
# THE DEBATE
# ABOUT READING

DEBATES about how and when to teach reading occupy considerably more space than debates about the teaching of mathematics or languages. For a long time past there has been little support in such debates for the position I have taken. For example, Dr Barbara Tizard wrote in the *Times Educational Supplement* in June 1977 about a survey of parent-teacher contact in six nursery schools. It was found that from 45 per cent to 78 per cent of the parents were teaching the children letters and numbers at home; others would have liked to do so, but were afraid of interfering and confusing the child. The teachers were critical of this activity.

> 'They thought the parents, instead of starting the children on the 3Rs, should be doing more for them in other directions, through providing stimulating conversation, books, and suitable toys.'

This has been the most usual attitude for a long time, but the ice is breaking up. Look back again at Professor Bruner's commendation of 'the style of care that increases the child's capacity to manage its own attention'. Then study the following paragraphs from *Children's Minds*, by Margaret Donaldson, published in 1978 with the blessing of Professor Bruner:

> Piaget's findings and arguments are complex, but one point that emerges very clearly is that *awareness* typically develops when something gives us pause and when consequently, instead of just acting, we stop to consider the possibilities of acting which are before us. The claim is that we heighten our awareness of what is actual by considering what is possible. We are conscious of what we do to the extent that we are

conscious also of what we do *not* do — of what we might have done. The notion of *choice* is thus central.

. . . We cannot expect to find any simple answer to such a momentous question — but observe how, here again, learning to read may have a highly significant contribution to make . . . the lasting character of the print means that there is time to stop and think, so that a child has a chance to consider possibilities — a chance of a kind he may never have had before.

Thus it turns out that those very features of the written word which encourage awareness of language may also encourage awareness of one's own thinking and be relevant to the development of intellectual self-control, with incalculable consequences for the development of the kinds of thinking which are characteristic of logic, mathematics and the sciences.

Well, if learning to read may encourage awareness of one's own thinking and be relevant to the development of intellectual self-control, it seems reasonable to start earlier rather than later. However, even if an early start were accepted (and Ms Donaldson does not decisively advocate this) there would remain several aspects of our preferred method which many teachers would find objectionable. In this chapter I want to consider each of these elements separately, as far as possible.

This preferred method is, as preceding chapters have shown, the *early* presentation of *three-dimensional capital letters*, identified *phonically* and encouraged *at home*.

## Early presentation

The first reason for encouraging an early start is enjoyment, both for children and parents. Building blocks, reading and painting give the best opportunities for visible achievement; sand and water give agreeable and useful experience but there is not much to show for it. At the age of two there is a great deal of satisfaction to be had from mastering a single letter, and much more from a single word. A single word has rich significance for a young child; they speak economically. Not so for a six-year-old. Even the sentences used in school texts are lifeless.

'Most British teachers expect their students to start the serious business of learning to read some time in their first or second school year, when the children are aged five or six.
. . . The carefully constructed reading primer is always an unsatisfacory compromise. Whether it depends on vocabulary control or phonic restriction, the child is being asked to read material he would never deliberately seek to listen to or say himself.' Asher Cashdan, *The Reading Teacher*, January 1973.

In contrast, I have a tape recording of Tinu's little son, when aged two and a half, puzzling out a set of picture cards; you can hear him still, saying 'C. .Ca. .Car. . .CARROT!' And the shout, 'I read it! I *read* it!'

Reading, however you define it, is a mysterious skill; it is most natural that children should acquire it at different rates. But the time available cannot be so easily extended forward from a late start; many authorities hold that children who are not reading easily at eight are not likely to become fluent readers. I suggest that an early start allows the symbols on which the whole structure is built to sink down into the depths of consciousness, so that it seems impossible to remember a time when 'S' didn't identify itself as 'Ssss'. The stages that follow, from sounding out 'SIT' to allowing 'sesquipidalian' to pour smoothly off the page into the mind, are able to build themselves up organically.

An important argument in favour of early reading is that it used to be common. Marjorie Fisher, in *Intent Upon Reading*, a commentary upon books suited to various purposes, remarks in passing that in the nineteen twenties books were mostly bought for children of reading families, who moved quickly from their primers to *The Wind in the Willows*. 'Nowadays,' she adds, 'among the countless thousands of children demanding books for first solo reading, there are many who read late, at six or seven instead of four or five.'

I could back that up with a selection of well known names, like the Bröntes and William Morris, whose reading at four or five is mentioned, though not as anything unusual. Instead I will content myself with one fine example: Thomas Arnold, 'a child who, at the age of three, had been presented by his father, as a reward for proficiency in his studies, with the twenty-four volumes of

Smollett's *History of England*.

Two studies of successful planned classes in early reading which I have found interesting are by Dr Rachel Cohen in a bilingual school in Paris *(L'Apprentissage Précoce de la Lecture)* and a report by William Fowler in *Interchange 2/2*. This journal is published by the Ontario Institute for Studies in Education.

John M. Hughes in *Reading and Reading Failure* gives a convenient summary of some research in this field to which I note frequent reference:

> Professor Durkin carried out an experiment at the University of Illinois which involved carefully controlled comparison of thirty children who had learned to read before six years with those who had learned to read later. By the end of the third year of schooling, the early readers were still one year ahead on average. Durkin found that all the parents of the early readers had noticed that their children had taken an interest in reading before the age of four. All these parents had assisted their children in identifying letters, numbers, words and sounds. But above all, they had spent time answering their children's many questions and discussing the meanings of words. The parents of late readers generally accepted that reading should be taught by a teacher in school. These parents were also too busy to respond to the possibility that their children were ready to learn to read.

**Three-dimensional**

Just another way of saying 'solid'. Anything flat, on a smooth surface of paper or any other material, is said to be two-dimensional; it has length and width. Anything solid has three dimensions, length, width and depth or thickness. Common sense tells us that a baby is more likely to take notice of a solid object he can touch than of lines on paper. However, they do take notice of marks on paper very early, so the 3-D element is not crucial, just helpful.

Russian studies have shown that children aged three who did not respond to squares and triangles shown on a screen learned to respond correctly after they had prolonged opportunity to feel and handle solid squares and triangles. A paper by E. Gibson gives further support to the common-sense assumption:

> Solid objects, which possess depth at their edges, are discriminated earlier than two-dimensional pictures or line drawings. If perceptual learning occurs in the earlier phase, it involves a discovery of invariant properties of the object which the stimulation itself specifies and which are critical for distinguishing one object from another. What is learned is learned in isolation from background or differentiation rather than an associative meaning for depth . . . Ability to discriminate those features of objects which are critical for identification may transfer to outline drawings such as letters, but some critical features of letters remain to be discriminated after four years of age. The process again is one of differentiation rather than with association. E. Gibson 'Development of perception: discrimination of depth compared with discrimination of graphic symbols. *Cognitive Development in Children* (Chicago 1970).

Further, I urge the possibility that children who have the chance to learn early, and using the sense of touch as well as sight, getting to know each letter familiarly, are less likely to emerge as dyslexic. The methods I propose are very like those that are used with children of six and seven who have been diagnosed as dyslexic. Here is part of a letter from Dr Graham Curtis Jennings, of Staines. I had seen him on television, explaining how he was able to identify children who were likely to be found, later, to be dyslexic. I wrote to him. He replied:

> 'You have of course hit the nail on the head in your approach, namely, to use a multisensory approach coupled with early introduction of reading material graduated to developmental ability.
>
> My problem in Ashford is that teachers are (i) ignorant of the possibility that some children might have a genetically determined disorder that prevents the acquisition of the skills of reading and writing and (ii) that even if they believe it exists I couldn't as a doctor know anything about it.
>
> So my job is to build bridges. I teach anybody who will listen to me; teachers, parents, doctors, nurses, health

visitors. I write about it, lecture, even appear on TV!

Until the climate in the teaching profession is right I dare not let parents go to teachers with their anxieties. If they do the teachers label them as worriers, trouble-makers, etc., and become defensive and even label the child as coming from an anxious household!. . .'

It seems to me also that if the early multisensory approach is helpful to potential dyslexics, it is also true that a family that is geared to early learning for ordinary children is in a favourable position to give any handicapped child who may turn up a better start than they would have otherwise.

A 'multisensory approach' might imply the association of sounds with colours or with music. My reliance is simply on solid objects which can be handled. It is obvious that these objects will be letters rather than words; a carved or moulded vocabulary would of necessity be limited. Which sort of letters, capital or lower case?

## Capitals

Capital letters are out of fashion. This is because 'whole words' are normally seen as the only possible starting point for reading. I shall return to the question of whole words and the reasons why they are favoured. For the moment, enough to say that the principle on which 'whole-word' teaching is based is that different words have different shapes. These shapes depend on the projections of different letters above or below the line of print in lower case. Whole words in capitals do not look as different from one another as do the same words in lower case; compare CAPITAL and CAPTAIN with 'capital' and 'captain'. Those who advocate a whole-words approach do not find capital letters acceptable. One result is that it has become quite difficult to buy sets of plastic capital letters; lower case can be found easily.

But *if* individual letters can be shown to be a practical choice, then capital letters have every advantage over lower case. They are the real letters, the forms into which the alphabet evolved over many centuries from the Phoenicians, through the Greeks, to the Roman perfection of Trajan's Column. Evolution required that they develop in such a way as to be easily distinguished one from the other.

Early Latin manuscripts were written in capitals. Gradually scribes in a hurry rounded angles, ran letters together. Different centres evolved different conventions in the matter of extending letters above or below the main line. The first printed letters were modelled on these manuscript letters. By now printing has developed a great variety of typefaces, all those that use what we still call the Roman alphabet following a uniform code, with 'f' rising above the line, 'j' descending. Designers of typefaces try to make letters that blend harmoniously with one another and which are legible when assembled into words.

The result is that lower-case 'c' and 'e' are more alike than are C and E; 'i' and 'l' more alike than I and L; m, n, h, r, resemble each other more closely than do M, N, H, R. By far the most confusing are the four, d, b, q, p, which are identical in shape but simply reversed or turned around.

Of course there are ways to tackle these difficulties. Those two of our children who were introduced to reading as instructed in the *Beacon Teacher's Manual* had trouble for a long time with 'b' and 'd'. I pointed out to them that the word 'bed' was rather the shape of a bed, and that they could think of this when confused. This still required them to find a remedy for a confusion which the others never experienced. What is more, it depended on having the written word in front of them. If you are offering a small child three-dimensional lower-case letters you have to give, in effect, four different names to the same object, as if you were to say that something was a scissors when the point was towards you, a shears when pointing away, with two other titles when facing right or left.

Nobody disputes the fact that capital letters are easier to distinguish than are lower case; the Bullock Report, *A Language for Life*, makes observations similar to mine; the paper by E. Gibson, referred to above, says that difficulty with rotation may continue until the age of eight.

Just as capital letters are easiest to identify, they are easiest to write; Marion Richardson's *Writing Patterns* perfect the writing of capitals before introducing continuous writing in lower case.

A further advantage is that if you can make a typewriter available the child will find capitals on the keyboard and will of course find it easier to know what he is doing if the machine is typing capitals as well. Later, a typewriter can help him to find which lower-case letter belongs to which capital.

Note, also, how often important messages are delivered in capitals:

DANGER     STOP     KEEP OUT
POISON     IN     OUT     PUSH

When children are taught capitals they have nothing to unlearn. In this there is a contrast with the initial teaching alphabet (i.t.a.). This most interesting scheme, which has been quite widely used in English schools, is made up of forty-four symbols, some identical with ordinary lower-case letters, the others different, each one representing no more than one sound, or phoneme. Since the English language provides so many problems this could be an important contribution to learning; the letters could, I suppose, be presented in solid form. There remains the difficulty that unless the whole community changes (which is not the aim of the designers) children have to drop it at some time and make the transition to ordinary letters. Some find this more difficult than others. I would claim, diffidently, that an early start with phonic capitals may be expected to get any child to the same point that might be expected from a school-age start with i.t.a. The possibilities of a two-year-old start with i.t.a. have not, so far as I know, been explored.

**Identified phonically**

Note that by this I mean simply that if you accept the argument of three-dimensional capital letters, a sound rather than a name is the economical way to identify them. The sooner the better. There is no real need for English letter names until you have to spell a word over the telephone and if two people are in the same room they can write the word down. Families reared phonically have no difficulty with Scrabble or∙'I spy'. There is plenty of time to learn the alphabet when reading is well established.

This may sound odd to parents. I have met adults who were actually at Montessori school and who had forgotten that they themselves learnt sounds before letter names. So, if you feel that it is mere crankiness to call a letter anything other than its name, I ask you to consider for a few moments the steps that must be taken by a beginner who has been taught the names: 'Pee says "puh", Ay says "ih", en says "n", so that word must be "pin".' Go through the same steps with *India, wagon, octagon,* then try sounding the letters instead; the second 'i' in India is a little different from the first, but neither of them is 'eye'. If you can remember the introduction of decimal coinage, you may recollect that for a long time we had to translate each ten pence into shillings in our heads; letter names are similar obstacles.

On this point anyway research results are clear. Dr John Downing (*Reading,* Vol. 8, No. 3) reports that three independent experimenters (Ohnmacht, 1969; Johnson, 1970; Samuels, 1971) have each tried this (the teaching of letter names) under rigorous scientific control and all reached the same conclusion — that letter-name teaching gives the child no help whatsoever in learning to read.

On the other hand, it is allowed that children who know the names often learn sooner than children who do not; the probable reason is that the former come from homes where there are books.

This warning about letter names is directed towards parents rather than teachers, who are not now likely to begin with anything but words. Though 'phonics' were undervalued or even ignored in schools for many years, I think we reasonably suppose that by now practice in many schools would resemble that recommended in John M. Hughes' excellent book, *Reading and Reading Failure*:

> When phonic teaching is based on a child's sight vocabulary and language experience, it means that he is taught to recognise whole words — for example, 'dog', before he is taught the sounds of the symbols 'd', 'o' and 'g'. At the beginning stage of reading, the word 'dog' is more meaningful than the three symbols from which it is formed. The foundation of phonics are established once the child has acquired a number of sight words and the teacher brings the child's attention to the sounds associated with the initial letters of these known words.

### Letters or words

Mr. Hughes' explanation of how to teach 'd' brings us back full circle to the question of whether children should be introduced to letters before words or words before letters. His case rests on the assumption that the word 'dog' is more meaningful than the three symbols of which it is formed. It all depends. In a household like ours, where 'D' was familiar since well before the age of two and was known to be Dada's letter, while even when there was a resident dog, or bitch, she was always referred to as Sherry, and dogs met outside might be rather alarming, the assumption is not valid.

(Incidentally, if we had tried to use three-dimensional *lower-case* letters 'd' would not have been simply DADA's letter; it would have been barbara's and pierce's and probably the queen's also).

The argument, as I have said, is circular. If you use phonic 3-D capitals, you can introduce them early; you can build up blending and reading very gradually, at an age when even single words are interesting; once phonically regular words are read easily, it is not difficult to introduce further letter clusters and even the most difficult pattern, the final 'E' that signals that the vowel before it is long. Once this lesson has been absorbed, the child is practically independent. Lower-case letters can be linked with their capital sources, and all that is needed is something interesting to read.

If you choose to teach words before you teach letters you lose the advantages of capital letters and of the multisensory approach. You rule out, by definition, the early teaching of lower-case letters as well as capitals. True, you hope, as we all do, that children will have books and hear them read aloud, but that is a common factor; I would expect it to accompany any attempt to teach reading. Beyond that, you are left with two alternatives, a 'reading readiness programme', listening to sounds, looking at shapes, and so on, all of which I believe to be included in our preferred method, or the encouragement of early recognition of whole words, 'sight words'.

In a casual way, such recognition is common. Peter Ustinov's mother has a funny little story about Peter, as a babe in arms, rousing a whole bus load of passengers with his excitement about the word OXO on a hoarding. Glen Doman, with his book *Teach Your Baby to Read*, made early recognition into a system.

It happened, as I have explained in the first part of this book, that I used this method with the last two children. Our experience was very like that of the mothers who replied to a small survey reported by Asher Cashdan in *Where?*, July 1968. Two-thirds of his sample enjoyed themselves; the children, average age two and a quarter, learnt single words easily and rapidly, but the further reading, about noses and toes, was not interesting.

We began with two children, age fifteen months and two and a quarter years. We had months of enjoyment, making jokes about snails and worms and members of the family. By the time they had a 'reading vocabulary' of about 120 words confusion and-frustration set in. New words often had roughly the same appearance as words they had learnt. Even though I had tried to introduce recognition of letter sounds from fairly early on, both were reluctant to use such clues. They resented the fact that the magic was fading; it was clear to them that the written word was something that should convey its meaning at a glance; they were unwilling to back-track.

Admittedly, both were reading quite competently at six and continued to be voracious readers but they were not as competent or as independent, or nearly as good at spelling, as their five siblings who made the smooth progression; letters, words, picture cards, then homemade books and a short time spent covering the series of Beacon Readers.

### The background to 'whole words'

If letters are the traditional introduction, and parents tend to teach them in spite of teachers' disapproval, why such almost universal emphasis on whole words in the English-speaking world? We have seen that teaching letter names does not help children, and that teaching names and sounds together does impose an extra burden, but why does not the educational establishment simply tell parents to use letter sounds? This used to puzzle me, until I came across *Reading and the Psychology of Perception,* by Hunter Diack, published in 1963. He explained that the idea of introducing children to reading by means of whole words instead of letters grew up in the United States between 1820 and 1840. This trend got a considerable boost from an investigation by J. McK. Cattell in 1885 which proved that adult readers could perceive only three or four *unrelated* letters during a brief exposure; if the letters were related, if they were words, the subjects could grasp up to twenty-four letters during the same exposure. This delivered a damaging blow to the alphabetic method of teaching. Diack says:

> Sixty years after Cattell's experiment some 10,000 books and articles about the teaching of reading could be found; in only

a negligible number of them was it suggested that children should learn letters before words.

Indeed, in 1974 Professor Patrick Groff of San Diego University wrote in *Reading* (Vol. 8, No. 4) that the invention called 'sight words' was in as high esteem as ever. He proceeds to undermine the system completely by showing that out of a list of 238 high-frequency words only twenty per cent have a shape of their own, not duplicated by some other frequently used words, e.g. nest, rest; drink, drunk; frock, knock.

Hunter Diack found that words did not have to be so close as that to permit confusion. In a classroom full of children who had been taught whole words he wrote *aeroplane* on the blackboard and they all cheerfully shouted *elephant*; it would seem that that large animal was the only long word on their flash cards.

In his book Diack mentioned that his own daughter had mastered most of the letters and begun to read words somewhere between two and three years of age. To support an article I was planning, I wrote to him and asked him why he had not continued and taught her to read. He replied that he did; that when she went to school at the usual age she was deliberately 'untaught'. His own word. Hunter Diack proceeded to write a phonically based Reading Scheme, *Royal Road Readers,* which I have several times seen commended.

If then the 'whole-word' theory is so mistaken, why does it persist? Partly, I suppose, because there is some truth in it. Nobody who has learnt to read spells out words; indeed, it seems that the upper half of a line of print provides all the clues we need. (Why, then, not teach children to recognise just the upper halves of words?) Then there is the defeatist belief that English spelling is so irrational that the only hope is to learn to recognise each word.

In Ireland at least teachers, until recently, were ignorant of the possibilities of phonics. I have come across several instances even in the late seventies, of remedial teachers who were carrying on their remedial work with the very same whole-word and spelling methods that had already baffled the children.

In the wider world, where at least phonics were debated, I suspect that Cattell's investigation may have been made at a crucial time, when teachers were coming to see themselves as professionals. The results were sanctified in training colleges, built into sets of readers; discussion of teaching methods was based on those readers, and so on. This is mere speculation. I have good evidence that it is taken for granted that the 'alphabetic method' is old fashioned. An article in *Reading* told about a visit by English teachers to schools in Finland. They found that teachers in Finland do not consider reading to be a problem. In the first eight weeks of school the class had read thirty-four pages of their reader (in capital letters) and had learnt the name and associated phonemes of thirteen letters of the twenty-one-letter alphabet. The last stories in the same reader had quite complex plots and a wide vocabulary. Yet the visitor's final comment is 'No one would advocate starting school at seven and *returning* to an alphabetic method . . . .' (My italics).

## Encountered at home

I have already argued at length in favour of home as the place for early learning and for early learning as a means to make life at home more enjoyable. It must be obvious that each of the steps or stages in reading that I have mentioned is far more easily managed by a parent who is in touch with his/her child for most of the day; letters, cards, homemade books, 'listen to me reading'. Experts say that it would be a good thing if first reading could be taught on an individual basis; they sometimes suggest that senior pupils should be brought into the classroom to 'hear' the younger children reading. Every now and then one reads some new discovery that children read better if parents 'hear' them at home. Hear reading selected by the teacher, of course.

At home reading can so easily be locked into real life; at home there is no need to consult a record chart to see just what each child is reading or what her problems are; at home it is almost always possible to drop everything when a learner demands a hearing. But the most important thing, to my mind, is that while a teacher who has taught fifty or five hundred children may still be delighted when number five-hundred-and-one cops on, she cannot be as delighted as a parent. And number five-hundred-and-one will be happy to be appreciated, but hardly as happy as when a 'significant other' enjoys her achievement along with her.

I attended the first European Conference of the International Reading Association, held near Paris in the spring of 1977. Here I picked up a great deal of interesting information. In regard to learning at home, I noted that nearly eight per cent of children in Finland may be expected to be reading fluently when they start school at seven, while another twenty-eight per cent have made a good start. In Madrid one quarter were usually fluent, another quarter familiar with the elements. Italian children start school at six; about thirty per cent were familiar with the elements. (They are taught by means of capital letters associated with pictures and are expected to have mastered the structure of the word within three months and to be ready to move on to cursive writing).

However, the sentence that I would have liked to bring home engraved on precious metal was thrown out in passing by Professor Merritt, of the Open University. He said, *'Any intelligent mother can teach her child to read better than any teacher.'*

One might alter this to read 'any intelligent *parent* . . .' In any event the sentence completes this chapter so fittingly that the following quotation, which I cannot allow to be wasted, must be seen simply as a footnote:

> In Sweden . . . the church Law of 1686 had made reading competence mandatory for marriage and participation in church ceremonies, such as the Last Supper. The parish priest examined all adults regularly, usually once a year, with regard to literacy and mastery of the scriptures. . .
>
> The literacy campaign was launched almost entirely without resort to formal schooling. In the last analysis the parents had the responsibility of seeing that the children learned to read, and the parents were controlled by the clergy. The overwhelming majority had achieved literacy in reading long before provisions for elementary schooling were made compulsory by legislation. Still some 25-30 years later about one-fifth to one-third of all children were taught at home, and children who entered elementary school were expected to have acquired some basic reading skills at home. . .
>
> Almost universal competence in reading can be achieved, given adequate motivation, in a pre-industrial society without formal schooling. (Thorsten, Husén, *The School in Question*, 1979).

*References— see page 128.*

# Chapter 11
# REFLECTIONS

**This chapter is concerned rather with a possible future than with the present or past; I have not therefore, been able to document every reference.**

IN THE first pages of this book I made a claim to have been rather far-sighted in taking up both early cognitive learning and de-schooling before either the phrase or the word had been invented. Now I feel the need to pull out some further evidence of my ability to sense the way in which the wind is going to change.

Almost the first interest that Sean and I shared was the desire for a more active role for the laity in the liturgy, this at a time when Irish Catholic congregations used to remain silent throughout Mass. That has changed, though not perhaps in exactly the way we hoped.

Next, as soon as we had a garden and a kitchen, we made compost, grew vegetables and baked wholemeal bread. It seemed impossible to buy wholemeal flour then, we sometimes ground our own; now there are three varieties in every grocery shop and supermarket.

A long pause, and I found myself in on the start of a whole series of campaigns: to encourage interest in Montessori; to get rid of corporal punishment in schools; to end obligatory Irish for the Leaving Certificate; to allow parents free visiting to children in hospital; to organise an interdenominational National School. The first Irish Family Planning Clinic was set up by a committee of five doctors and myself — some of us had met through the corporal punishment campaign. All of these endeavours have been reasonably successful; early this year (1982) corporal punishment was banned in Irish schools by the Minister for Education, Mr. John Boland.

My energies, such as they are, have been focused during the last two years on spreading knowledge in Ireland of the international language, Esperanto. Results have not been spectacular, but I trust that its rapidly growing importance in the rest of the world will make an impression here also.

The reason I call up all these credit-items is to avert the wrath of other women, especially women journalists, who are bound to believe that someone who rejects not only creches and nursery schools but even ordinary primary school is hell-bent on bringing back female slavery. Listen, sisters, I am not a one-woman support system for patriarchy. I have not made a bed or ironed a shirt for any of my sons since they were about eight. I am even a good trade unionist; I was Branch Secretary of the Dublin Freelance Branch of the National Union of Journalists for three years and did my share to get more money for other women as well as men. I resigned because I had to look after my ninety-four-year-old mother; she is a woman, too; who else could I expect to take her on?

Well, I *would* like to remove the need for group child-care; I believe that a change in that direction will come soon. Remember that half of the babies who will then be looked after by their favourite person will be girls; think of their side of the question, and read on.

Two recent articles in *The Guardian,* a British paper which is well known for its support of women's rights, suggest a totally satisfactory system of day-care is hardly possible. In one it was reported that a nursery in central London which gave very good care, allowing parents to work full time, was about to fold up because the premises, which had been provided rent free, were about to close. *Rent-free,* it was costing £300 per month per child. Employers were prepared to contribute only on behalf of unusually valuable employees. The organisers are reported to have said that 'child-care with small staff/child ratios should not be thought of as cheap'.

The second article (18 February 1982) examined conditions in Sweden, where for the last ten years government policy, in response to women's demands, has been to create conditions which would make it easier for married women to be part of the labour force. In 1972 the Family Policies Committee said:

There should be only three sets of circumstances when a parent is obliged to remain at home: when a child is born; when the child is sick, and if a severely handicapped child must be at home. Only then will maintenance support be payable.

The result, it seems, is that women have to put their children into private (black-market) child-care, which is much more expensive, because the queues for subsidised care are too long. Women say they are trying to live up to an impossible ideal.

Typical sufferers were interviewed. Anita, principal of a nursery school and day-care centre, said that though she had the support of the man she lived with and though she had child-care organised, she still had to work from six in the morning to midnight, 'I bring work home — and there's the children, supper, housework. I never have time to watch TV . . .'

Poor Anita, minding other people's children, while strangers mind hers and both apparently subsidised by the state. No wonder women out at work are catching up men's heart-failure death-rate. But the reason the Swedish government is worried is that the birth rate has been going down spectacularly.

This does not seem surprising; I met the same pattern years ago at a Planned Parenthood conference in Finland. Everything in that country was marvellously organised; mothers did not need to stay at home even if their child was sick; thoroughly trained substitutes would take over. Despite these services the birth rate there was running below replacement.

Day-care, even when it is as carefully planned as this, does not relieve mothers of all their problems and there is plenty of evidence also that it is not as good for the children as even moderately good parenting. Professor J. McVicar Hunt, in a paper given in 1972, compared babies from 'families of poverty' whose mothers had taken part in a motherhood training programme with four other groups of babies and children up to the age of four. Two of the groups of children were in orphanages of different types, one group was mainly in day-care, and the last was made up of home-reared babies from middle-class families in Massachusetts. The first group, raised by the trained mothers, showed themselves steadily ahead of *all* the others in a series of standard tests of sensorimotor development; the average for this group at the age of one year and five months was two years in advance of the worst orphanage, and five months ahead of the middle-class children. Evaluating a number of Head Start programmes, Uri Bronfenbrenner found that lasting gains were made only when parent and child were *both* involved in cognitively challenging tasks.

A Hungarian director of a bureau of child-care told researchers that she could not understand why a rich nation like the USA should wish to inflict on its children the group care of which a poor nation like Hungary was trying to rid itself. (See Moore, R. S.). From London, Dr Barbara Tizard reported that children ask ten times as many questions at home as in nursery school. Why then are so many women so anxious to work outside the home when their children are small? Money comes first, I suppose; then loneliness and boredom. Other women, not so many, are concerned about missing steps on the career ladder, or may be intensely devoted to their work.

Money has a double role; the woman's wage may be needed to keep an expensive roof over the family's head; even if this is not so she may feel she needs money to keep her self-respect. Having been in the habit of earning her own living, she finds it painful to have to take money from her children's father. Money should solve some problems.

In several countries in Eastern Europe mothers are paid about ninety per cent of the average wage for three years if they stay at home. 'To stay at home and educate a child is at least as valuable as to work in a factory,' a Bulgarian delegate told my discussion group at an International Planned Parenthood Conference. It is an idea which has been taken up by the Childminders' Union in Ireland. But money paid to mothers is a limited solution.

I much prefer the step proposed in various forms, and under different names, by a number of responsible economic thinkers. It may be called National Dividend, National Transfer, National Income Scheme. One exponent, Dr James Albus, director of the NASA Artificial Intelligence Programme, says in *People's Capitalism* that there are no economic problems, including those resulting from the world's exploding population, which are beyond our present physical and technical capacity to solve, but that to realise our true potential we must somehow reorganise our system of rewards, incentives and methods of wealth distribution. Common to his scheme and to the others is the transfer from the exchequer to each citizen, at the age of about eighteen, of a minimum income, equal at least to current unemployment benefit, but which would allow and encourage the recipient to work and earn as well. Along with this would go a realistic children's allowance.

Now that I have discussed one such scheme with groups of people whom I would have expected to appreciate it, I have discovered that many find it quite shocking. If I were to debate the matter here this chapter would get out of hand. I can only recommend US readers to get hold of Albus, British readers to write to the Ecology party, 36/38 Clapham Road, London SW9, asking for *Working For a Future*. (Incidentally, the Ecology Party of Ireland is at Washington Lodge, Grange Road, Rathfarnham, Dublin 14.) Irish readers may wish to get publication No. 37 of the National Economic and Social Council, *Integrated Approaches to personal Income Taxes and Transfers* by Brendan Dowling. For everyone Keith Roberts, (bibliography).

For the moment, then, forget about the economics and the ethics of the scheme, just imagine the effect on someone born when the scheme is functioning. When she is a baby, her mother is nearly always within reach. In my version anyway, she naturally picks up skills in the way outlined in the rest of this book. The difference is that if mother feels the need of company or support the two of them can drop in to a Parent and Child Centre where they will meet other parents, with children of various ages, who are also free to visit the Centre instead of rushing off to factories or offices. Friends can meet, children can mix or not as they wish, but they cannot be bullied by tougher kids — they cannot be bullies either. So how is this for a flight of fancy?

Perhaps a brother or sister joins the family. We had better give the first one a name, say, Anna. She likes music. Her father plays several instruments and loves to help the children, so mother and father decide each to work a three day week, so that he can see more of the children. Other kids sometimes come in for music. (In a different scenario, father is an alcoholic, but since Mother and Anna have adequate incomes they are able to move out. This is not a novel, so we will not find out whether the shock brings him to AA).

When Anna is ten, she goes to class during the morning. Some afternoons she helps in a local shop. When she is twelve her mother goes back to study part-time; Anna and her brother can by now do a lot of the work about the house and garden.

During her teens she follows up a growing interest in musical instruments. She studies history, maths, physics and chemistry at the nearest Community College. She manages to be taken on as assistant, then apprentice, by an instrument maker who pays her a small wage. Every week she babysits for a handicapped child, every autumn works in an international forestry workcamp; she is interested in trees because she works with wood. Now she is eighteen. She is a citizen, with the income of a citizen. She feels more responsibility for her neighbourhood. She will live at home for another couple of years, making a fair contribution; her father is now about forty, and thinks it is time for a sabbatical. Remember even when he leaves his job he has his basic income. I think his plan is to travel a bit buying materials and selling the instruments made . by the small firm that Anna and a friend are going to set up. He may also spend more time teaching music in the neighbourhood classes, since he has found that children like to learn with him.

Perhaps I should try to write a novel sometime; I find myself quite curious about the father; what work did he do? Was he an industrial chemist, or was he a bus driver? I know mother was a radiographer; what did she choose to study? I must remind myself that the point of the narrative was that neither Anna nor her family had to be anxious; neither she nor her parents would ever be unemployed in the way that people are under present systems. Even if she had not found such an attractive career, the psychological effect of achieving the income of a citizen would be very different from that of drawing the 'Dole', though the amounts involved might be similar.

Note that there is nothing fantastic about the rest of the story. Much of the work of the world has always been done, often enjoyed, by people of twelve or fourteen. In the Basque co-operative of Mondragon, in Northern Spain, the students in the technical school own their own school, the school owns a factory for electrical goods, the students work in the factory for half the day, study for the other half, and so maintain both themselves and their school. Schools in Tanzania and China feed themselves.

Then, I said that Anna went to class when she was ten. In *Better Late Than Early* (see bibliography) Raymond and Dorothy Moore, both highly qualified in the world of education, assemble quantities of research to show that children under eight develop better outside school. The younger child is too much subject to peer pressure, too little able to stand on his own feet. Different capacities develop at different rates; IML, 'integrated maturity

110

level', is not reached, they say, until between the ages of eight and ten.

I accept that by that age there may be benefit in learning with others, provided the groups are small, not more than twelve. I have implied that music would be a subject for study together. Other useful information, such as nutrition, anatomy, elementary geography, a common fund of poetry, and some skill in locating information, could be acquired easily by children already literate and numerate. Access to computer terminals would presumably be important. (See *Mindstorms*, Papert). At least equally important would be the opportunity to work with a skilled adult.

I trust that with this sketch of the lives of Anna and her mother I have suggested a satisfactory option for a mother who, as things are, might work outside the home because of needing money or because of being lonely. I have neglected the other problem; women who are concerned about progress in specially interesting careers. Given the opportunity, I would ask them whether they had any plans for taking on a second responsible, time-consuming job alongside the principal one. If that would be absurd, why take on a child? Is it not sufficient luck (reward?) to have a really interesting job? Or they might reflect on the extension of active life made possible by Hormone Replacement Therapy. But the best hope would be the erosion of the whole competitive career structure, both for men and women, by the National Transfer.

It is not possible to pursue the questions of work, income and education any further in these pages. Instead, may I recommend three books, and conclude with two quotations.

The books are *News from Nowhere* by William Morris, a classic, in its time thought fanciful but now seen as in many ways practical; *Architect or Bee?* by Mike Cooley, winner of the 1981 Alternative Nobel Prize; *The Descent of Woman* by Elaine Morgan; in the present context, it's the final chapters of this splendid book that are most relevant.

Elaine Morgan borrowed some of her ideas and information from Professor I. Eibl-Eidesfeldt's book, *Love and Hate*. He is Director of the Human Ethology section of the Max Planck Institute, a successor to Tinbergen and Konrad Lorenz. I offer one of the paragraphs from his conclusion:

The means of bonding have always remained fundamentally

the same and they are in origin essentially derived from the behaviour patterns that bind mother and child. The mother-child relationship was historically — and still is in the development of the individual — the nucleus of crystallization for all social life. This relationship is already an individualized one in many higher mammals, probably so as to prevent danger of babies being exchanged which might put the rearing of the young at risk for a number of reasons. Our clear disposition to establish personal bonds has its roots here. It is innate to us. From the personal mother-child relationship we evolve the 'basic trust' from which our fundamental attitude of sociability then evolves and hence a general commitment. For these reasons attempts to prevent the growth of such family ties are highly questionable. What has to be done is to strengthen our trust in fellow men who are not known to us and this starts in the family. Only in this way do we evolve that social responsibility which is a prerequisite for a peaceful communal existence and probably indeed for our future existence as a species.

# Chapter 12
# RESOURCES

BEFORE I explain how to make or otherwise obtain the 'didactic material' to which I have referred in earlier chapters I must insist that the most important resource is Montessori herself. Her method is not simply one of using special objects but one of respecting children's thinking. This book is a description of one family's way of profiting from her insight. Anyone who finds it attractive and is willing to invest some time in offering their children similar opportunities should go to the source and read Dr Montessori's own description of how she pursued her discoveries simply by observing the children. When reading her book *The Montessori Method* one has to make some allowances for the lapse of time since it was written and for the fact that her children had had very restricted experience during infancy. *A Modern Approach to Montessori* by Paula Polk-Willard helps the reader to appreciate the originality and the lasting value of her discoveries. It should be remembered also that Maria Montessori was a powerful campaigner for women's rights until her time was entirely taken up by the struggle for the rights of children.

**Alphabetic list of material**

BOOKS
One learns to read in order to enjoy books; perhaps one enjoys books and therefore learns to read. It would be useless to make a list of favourite books which parents might not be able to find. We were so attached to a very small book, *A Boy Went Out to Gather Pears*, beautifully illustrated, that we borrowed it over and over again from the library, brought it in to a bookshop so that our order would be exact, but it never arrived. I will, then, mention just a few that should be available anywhere there are children's books, plus a few special favourites.

Nursery rhymes, of course; Benn, Oxford University Press and Blackie are three publishers of very satisfactory collections. Also of course, Grimms' fairytales. Maurice Sendak: *Alligators All around,* and others. *Winnie-the-Pooh* and *The House at Pooh Corner* are indispensable, so far as we are concerned; available in Latin and in Esperanto as well, delightful in both. A little older, six and upwards, all the books of Laura Ingalls Wilder; the Narnia books by C. S. Lewis (Puffin); the stories of E. Nesbit, especially *Five Children and It.* If you do not live near a bookshop you will find that Holt Associates, 729 Boylston St., Boston MA 02116 will send books promptly from an admirable selection. I recommend them to parents on both sides of the Atlantic.

Special favourites, not so easily available: *The Adventures of Rasselas, Prince of Abyssinia,* by Samuel Johnson; *Irish Fairy Tales,* James Stephens (Gill & Macmillan); *Celtic Wonder Tales,* Ella Young (Talbot Press, Dublin & T. Fisher Unwin, London).

A family favourite: *What-a-Mess and the Cat Next Door,* by Frank Muir, illustrated by Joseph Wright. (Benn.)

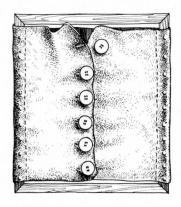

BUTTON FRAME

The original frames include sets of hooks and eyes, laces and other fastenings no longer much used. I made one frame, as illustrated, with large buttons, one with small and one with large patent-fasteners because they give a satisfying click.

Buckles and laces need practice but are not so easy to attach to frames; I used to encourage work with real sandals and shoes. A doll with multiple fastenings might be satisfactory. Each fastening should be demonstrated very slowly, step by step.

## COLOUR-FACTOR SET

This set of blocks is described in *Chapter Eight*. I could say a great deal more in an endeavour to show how remarkably it can enable the average parent to give any child that understanding of fundamental mathematical concepts which can so easily be missed when early work in arithmetic is based on written figures or counting and 'taking away' separate objects. Unfortunately the picture is not entirely rosy. The set of blocks can be obtained easily enough in Britain and in Ireland, in the former from the manufacturer, E. J. Arnold & Sons, Reading, Berks and presumably from other educational suppliers, in Ireland from School Supply Centre, Unit 13, Rathfarnham Shopping Centre, Dublin 14. The books are another matter.

*The Basic Colour-Factor Guide* by the designer of the Set, Seton Pollock, was published by Heinemann Educational Books; it makes quite stiff reading and is not planned directly for use with children. It should be read if obtainable.

The series of workbooks and parents' and teachers' manuals, *Colour-Factor Mathematics* by H. A. Thompson, which we found so enjoyable and enlightening, was discontinued after the introduction of decimal coinage. Problems involving shillings and pence, feet and inches, naturally appeared in most of the workbooks and were no longer relevant. However, there are only two pages with any questions of that sort in the first three books, the ones that lay the most important foundations. When two families of grandchildren needed them I wrote to the publishers, Messrs Heinemann, and they told me they had no plans to re-issue the books and that publication rights reverted to the author, with whom they put me in touch. He kindly provided the copies we needed, but he has very few more. I therefore urge interested parents to write either to Messrs Heinemann or to me (care of publisher). I would of course be particularly pleased to hear from anyone in a position to reprint these exceptional books. I must stress again that it is not simply a question of short steps and clear and pleasing diagrams; the language in which the books are written addresses the child as an intelligent individual and is ideally suited to develop independent study.

Meanwhile, I am glad to say that it is possible to buy two booklets called *Know Your Tables* by the same author, published in 1979. One is a workbook, the other a handbook for parents and teachers. They are designed to help children (or persons of any age) learn about the structure of numbers and their relation to other numbers. In traditional multiplication tables there are at least 132 different answers to be memorised; in this approach, only nineteen simple basic products need to be committed to memory. As companions to Colour-Factor, these booklets would be the next best thing to the original series. They are also published by Heinemann.

## CUPS AND PYRAMIDS

Cups, boxes, barrels, towers; plastic objects which can be fitted into each other in series or piled up in order are very widely available. Wooden versions are not so common but are, I think, preferable. Start off by giving just two or three items; make sure that when the play is over the things are arranged in order, because that is what they are designed for; if you want to use nesting cups in the sandpit, have a separate set.

## CYLINDERS

These are probably the most original and valuable source of activity in Montessori's 'didactic apparatus'. I suppose them to be the ancestors of all the plastic nesting cups and barrels our children play with. As she says in her book, they are very much like the case of weights used by a chemist. There are three blocks of wood fifty-five centimetres long, eight centimetres wide. In each block there are ten holes into which can be fitted corresponding cylinders of

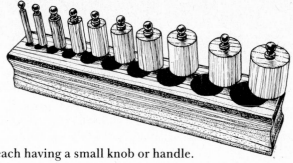

wood, each having a small knob or handle.

In one set of cylinders the largest is five and a half centimetres in height, two and a half in diameter, the smallest, one centimetre in height and in diameter, the others graded in between. This is the easiest set to put in place. Another set has cylinders all of equal height, varying only in diameter, the third set are all of the same diameter but graded according to height. (See illustration).

Until you have watched a child concentrating on the task of taking out, mixing and replacing one set, or all at the same time, and the intense satisfaction with which he or she sits back when the last one has settled into its right place, you do not know the meaning of the phrase 'the beauty of order'. It is a wonderful sight. However, the cylinders should be available at the right time, not too soon, not too late — for experienced children, about eighteen months. They should be treated with ceremony — not just whipped out and shoved in hit-and-miss.

For a couple of years I was one of a team of neighbours who helped out with a brain-damaged little boy who was following the Doman regime. I lent one block of cylinders to his mother. She told with joy that they were the first task he had ever undertaken independently; he found them in one room, put them in place and pushed the whole thing in to the next room to show her.

Unfortunately the full set is expensive; at the time of writing each block costs about IR£25.00 The various substitutes on the market can be used in a similar way, and provide very useful subjects for conversation. The authentic cylinders can be obtained from Association Montessori Internationale, 161 Konigennenweg, Amsterdam. In Ireland, they are available from Halo Supplies, 40 Main Street, Rathfarnham, Dublin 14.

### DRAWING AND PAINTING MATERIALS
Charcoal can be bought from an artists' colourman or collected from the garden bonfire. Buy only good crayons. Coloured pencils

117

make insets more enjoyable. Ball-points of all sorts are easy to use, but I think fibre-tips are rather *too* easy, and the marks they make are difficult to remove. A child who has got used to having a brilliant fibre-tip pen may not want to bother using a paint brush.

Paint brushes should be substantial; school fitches or the smallest sizes of household brushes. Small jars of poster paint are not much use; get powder colour or the containers of liquid paint sold for schools. One colour first, then two; I suggest red, then white and yellow, so that painter can mix pink or orange. Next, small jars with one brush for each colour. It is important to place brush in baby's hand so that it is held well up the shaft, between thumb and fingers, not gripped by four fingers in fist. If this is done from the beginning there is no difficulty. The only instruction needed is 'Don't squash the brush'.

DRESSING UP
Any household with a child in it should have a box or basket to hold a collection of old skirts, jackets, curtains, caps, scarves, necklaces and so on. Do you know how to burn the end of a cork to make a moustache and beard?

ESPERANTO
Esperanto is to language learning as Colour-Factor is to learning mathematics — but while the coloured blocks are left behind after childhood and only the concepts remain, the international language continues to be of use everywhere and for any purpose.

Esperanto was invented a hundred years ago — the first grammar was published by the inventor, Ludovic Lazarus Zamenhof, in 1887. It is a flimsy pamphlet, some twenty pages with a folded sheet listing root-words; to look from that to the collection of new books, journals, magazines printed every month in a hundred different countries; the United Nations office, the technical publications office in Budapest, the Graphic Centre in Rotterdam, the *Complete Works of Zamenhof* published in Japan — it's like picking up a dry little beech-nut and then looking up at the towering beech tree overhead.

For our present purpose there are three or four points I want to make. First, Ludovic was only a little boy of five when he first thought that if everyone understood one language there would be peace; second, he was still only a schoolboy of sixteen when he worked out the basis on which he built up the language. It is completely regular, therefore astonishingly easy to learn, yet completely flexible, able to express anything you want to say; beautiful, too. Children who learn it profit in two ways; they can within a month or so correspond with people all over the world; if they are able to travel they can join in youth camps and talk with other children of entirely different background; even if they do not wish to do either, but simply to read, they will come to understand grammar in a way that will make it very much easier not only to learn any other language but to grasp the structure of their own language.

Parents who want to teach it, who realise the value of being conscious of language but do not feel confident enough to teach any irregular language like French or German or Latin, can quite easily learn enough in a couple of months to enable them to start teaching the child and keep ahead until he or she is able to continue independently. China is the best source of books for younger children, and also of a monthly colour magazine which is wonderful value.

*Addresses:*
Esperanta Sekcio de Centro de Ĉinaj Eldonaĵoj,
(Guoji Shudian) PO Kesto 313, Beijing, China.

Esperanto Association of Ireland,
9 Templeogue Wood, Dublin 12.

Esperanto-Centro,
140 Holland Park Avenue, London W11 4UF.

Esperanto-Ligo por Norda Americo,
PO Box 1129, El Cerrito, CA 94530, USA.

For other countries, enquire from:
Universala Esperanto-Asocio,
Nieuwe Binnenweg 176, 3015 BJ Rotterdam, Netherlands.

## FIRE

There is general enthusiasm for enabling children to play with earth (in the form of sand), air and water, but the fourth traditional element, fire, is hardly considered except as it tops candles on birthday cakes. Fire was very significant in the development of the human race; I think children should be allowed to make themselves familiar with it. Our youngest found it particularly attractive and he had a little 'burning dish' in which he was allowed to light very small fires in the kitchen so long as I was there with him.

## GEOMETRICAL INSETS

These can be made as soon as you like. What is needed is a sheet of plywood thick enough not to curl up, of about thirty-six inches by eighteen. This can be divided handily into eighteen squares, out of which you can cut the shapes, giving yourself some leeway for mistakes.

Draw the geometrical shapes as illustrated. To cut them out you need a fretsaw with spare blades, a support, and a G-clamp to hold the support to a table. You need also a fine drill to make the first hole. A hobbies supplier should be able to provide these and show you how to use them, or indeed give you the name of someone with a power-saw who might make them for you. Once they are made

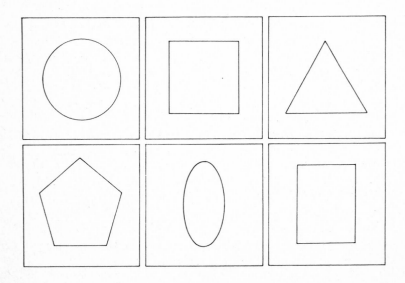

and sandpapered, glue a suitable handle to the centre of each, and seal with polyurethane or gloss paint.

In present-day Montessori schools metal insets are used; these can be obtained from suppliers listed.

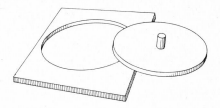

## LETTERS

Three-dimensional capital letters were the key to our preferred way of teaching reading. First time round we had no difficulty in buying plastic alphabets in capitals for very little money. When the time came to provide something for Ivan and the rest of the grandchildren things had changed; practically everything plastic was in lower case. However, we found that Galt Toys make an alphabet of large wooden letters, very suitable, and the Fisher-Price range of toys includes a desk with a set of plastic capitals which attach themselves magnetically to the desk. When not in use they are stored in a moulded tray with a space fitting each letter. This arrangement is excellent; it may seem a little expensive but the desk we got for Ivan has now supported two families of cousins, six children so far. (I must add that Ivan learnt while his mother was working full-time as a gardener, keeping him with her; what is more, until he heard the tape of his two-year-old self reading 'carrot', he took it for granted that he had learnt to read at school, though in fact at age five school said his reading age was nine).

I have heard of letters cut from polystyrene foam or from sponge; it has occurred to me that it would be quite easy to make some out of Play-doh and bake them slowly; baked Play-doh is amazingly tough.

The sandpaper letters are essential to Montessori's introduction to reading. Her children were older; I did not find that babies of eighteen months were interested in feeling sandpaper. We made a set of letters and used them as a support for writing practice. Manufacture was simple. A sheet of hardboard was sawn into rectangles, about six inches by eight or six by ten. These are painted with gloss paint, different colours each side. Meanwhile on some sheets of fine sandpaper you copy in chalk the letters from the Richardson *Writing Patterns,* both capitals and lower case, and cut around the chalk line, leaving a substantial outline suitable for feeling with one finger. The lower-case letters a, c, should be about two and a half inches high, the rest in proportion. Stick capitals on one side, matching lower case on the other; naturally all the capitals will be on backgrounds of the same colour. Some people might care to use four different colours, so as to be able to distinguish the vowels, a, e, i, o, u, from the consonants.

Children must be shown patiently how to trace the letters with one finger of their writing hand, right or left as the case may be, while holding the board with the other.

## LOGO

It seems that computers, especially mini-computers, are beginning to play an important part in education. It is not at all certain that everything that is now being done with computers in school is productive. Just before this book went to the printer Oliver has had the opportunity to do a short course in Logo at Edinburgh University, and we have had an Apple II, equipped with Logo, at home for a week or so. Logo is a language designed to enable children to learn computer programming — almost to teach themselves. It is also the only language designed specifically for learning; other languages have different purposes, and one picks them up as best one can while aiming at some other end.

Oliver has had the most experience and he thinks very highly of Logo; he says his own introduction to computers in University would have been much smoother, time would have been saved, if it had been available instead of his being thrown into Pascal right away. We have read about children of eight or so using Logo and the possibilities seem very interesting. (See Papert, *Mindstorms* in bibliography, also *Byte,* August 1982). Our computer scientist, Dr Alasdar Mullarney, played Devil's Advocate. He said that real computer programming is arduous work, for which there will be less and less need in the future; he sees no point in bringing half-baked programming into schools. On the other hand we argued that the elements of programming are also the elements of logical thinking, and the use of a computer might make families less dependent on schools. This last he thought an acceptable argument, and he has promised to have another look at Logo; of one thing he is certain, as are many others; that it is quite a mistake to introduce children to Basic, just because it is available.

It seems to me, from the slight vicarious and immediate experience that I have had, that Logo is an appropriate sequel to Montessori and Colour-Factor, and I hope I will be able to provide it at least for the grandchildren by the time they are about eight. Papert is now working in a World Computer Centre in France and there are plans to make wide provision for the children.

## MUSICAL INSTRUMENTS

We used only xylophone, piano, triangle, various sorts of drums and Alasdar's mouth-organ. Some of the children learnt recorder in school; it is well suited to home learning. Many homemade instruments are described in *The Playgroup Book* (see Porcher).

## 'RATTLEY BOXES'

Any containers that can be held and shaken will serve. It must be possible to distinguish two sets of them by different colours or markings. The most convenient I found were orange and yellow coloured aluminiuim tubes that had contained large tablets of vitamin C. Take six of each colour. Into one of each colour put a little sand, replace the screw top; use sticky tape or an adhesive to make sure that the child will not unscrew the tops and pour sand around. Make some small mark for your own information; it may not be so easy as you expect to distinguish one sound from another. Into the next pair put, say, some rice; into another, beans; into another, perhaps a few nails, or stones or wooden clothes-pegs, anything that makes a distinct sound.

Sort out the set yourself before trying it on the child. Arrange the orange tubes in a row. Take one yellow one, shake it beside your ear; then take the orange ones in turn, shaking each, until you find the sound that matches the one you have. When you find a pair, put them back in their box, or somewhere out of the way. Then find another pair by the same procedure.

This exercise is useful in two ways. It trains the hearing; we found a definite benefit later. It seems that this sort of matching also has importance in intellectual development, or so I gather from Papert's *Mindstorms.*

I think it best to begin with just three, or even two, pairs of containers.

READING CARDS

To make these you will need a pack of plain postcards, some coloured fibre-tip pens and eventually a list of suitable words.

The first words will be easy to think of; the names of five or six objects which you can draw recognisably and which are spelt with three letters. The illustration shows PEG, FAN, JUG, PIN, BOX, PAN. If possible include a 'catch' like PIN and PAN. Write the word in capital letters at the bottom of the card. Make two cards for each object. Cut the word off the bottom of one card on each matching pair. Re-read Chapter Four for description of game.

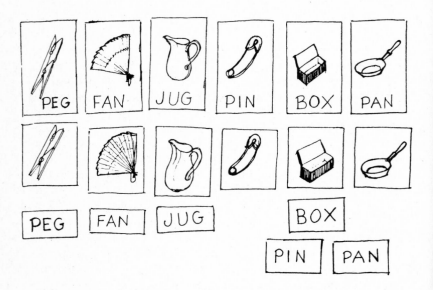

Once the game is going well you may find it helpful to have a progressive list of 'phonic' words. Our source was a set of Beacon Readers. Alternatives are the teacher's book for Fuzzbuzz Readers or *Sounds and Words* by V. Southgate and J. Havenhand (University of London Press Ltd.). Meanwhile, a few suggestions to keep you supplied:

VAN, CAR, BUS, LORRY, DOOR, WINDOW.
MOON, ZOO, TOOTH, STOOL, STICK, FOOT.
WINDOW, OWL, TOWN, TOWER, COW, TOWEL.

(You might like to include a picture of a comic foot stepping on a drawing-pin — 'OW!').

BROWN, RED, GREEN, PINK, BLACK, YELLOW.
SHIP, SHOP, DISH, SPLASH, CRASH, SHEEP.

And so on. But you do not have to compress the whole English spelling system onto cards. They are just starters.

Beacon Readers are published by Ginn & Co, Aylesbury (first impression 1922, fifty-seventh impression 1978).

SEWING

Sewing seems to suit four-year-olds best but there is no rule that says you cannot try it earlier. All you need is a packet of carpet needles, very thick and short, with very large eyes and rounded points. A lorry or a house drawn on a postcard is the next step. Make holes all along the outline about a quarter of an inch apart with the needle or a sharper instrument. Thread the needle with darning wool, heavy embroidery thread or fine string — anything that will pull through easily. Show the pupil how to bring the thread up from below, down from above and when they have got the whole way around, they can go around again, filling in the spaces. Quite soon you can show them the time-saving, useful backstitch. Do not forget to collect different fabrics for feeling. An interest in texture goes along with embroidery.

TEMPERATURE MATCHING

Empty aluminium screw-top containers from the chemist are very suitable and easy to come by. Take four. Fill one with iced water, one with water as hot as you can bear to hold. In the others, one part hot, two parts cold; two parts hot, one part cold. If you have eight jars, do two of each and arrange a master-set yourself, saying 'Hot, warm, cool, cold.' Let the child do the same, matching by feel.

Write the words on cards.

## WORKBOOKS

Ronald Ridout's *English Workbooks* are published by Ginn & Co. To adults they do not look exciting but our children enjoyed them.The information needed for answers is available on the same page as the questions. With their help parents can teach logical construction and the conventions of written English without having to criticise spontaneous communication. We used to offer the *First Introductory Workbook* about age five, then let the children continue at their own pace. I have seen the books in use in two schools but their introduction had been delayed and they did not offer any challenge. Consequently the children were just filling time.

## WRITING AND WRITING PATTERNS

Marion Richardson's *Writing and Writing Patterns* includes a Teacher's Book and six writing and tracing books. Read the Teacher's Book. Greaseproof sandwich bags, widely sold, are the right size to fit over the books for tracing. Now published by Hodder and Stoughton (27th impression).

**Bibliography**

Albus, Dr James, *People's Capitalism*, Maryland 1976. Library of Congress catalog card number 75-44585.

*Beacon Readers*, See 'Resources', Reading Cards.

Bronfenbrenner, U.S.A., 'A Report on Longitudinal Evaluations of Pre-School Programmes,' Washington 1974. See under Clarke & Clarke, *Early Experience, Myth or Reality*. London 1976.

Beekman, Daniel, *The Mechanical Baby*, Lawrence Hill & Co., Westport, Conn. 1977.

Bruner, Jerome, *Towards a Theory of Instruction*, Harvard 1966.
*Relevance of Education*, Penguin Education, London 1974.

Bullock, A. *A Language for Life*, HMSO 1975.

Clarke & Clarke, *Early Experience, Myth or Reality*, London 1976.
This useful book argues that later good experience can compensate for early bad experience, and gives many examples. But in each case the cure demands extra resources. The book includes a summary of the report by Bronfenbrenner (see above) which concludes that intervention has lasting effect only when parents are involved, and says 'not only does the child learn from the mother, the mother learns from the child'.

Cohen, Dr Rachel, *L'Apprentissage Précoce de la Lecture*. Presse Universitaire de France, Paris 1978.

Corcoran, T., Articles in *Irish Monthly*, Dublin 1924.

Culverwell, Professor E. F., *The Montessori Method*, George Bell & Sons, London 1912.

Dally, Ann, *Inventing Motherhood*, Burnett Books, London 1982. The author is historian, mother and practising psychiatrist as well.

Dantzig, Tobias, *Number, The Language of Science*, London 1938. Enticingly written history of mathematical thought.

Deakin, Michael, *The Children on the Hill*, André Deutsch. London 1974. An outside observer's view of intensive home learning; rather intimidating.

Diack, Hunter, *Reading and the Psychology of Perception*, Nottingham 1963. *Also* Daniels and Diack, *Royal Road Readers*. A phonic series often commended.

Donaldson, Margaret, *Children's Minds*, Fontana, London 1978. If you speak to children in their own language, you may find that they understand more than Piaget recognised.

Douglas, J. W. B., *The Home and the School*, A Study of Ability and Attainment in the Primary School; McGibbon & Kee, London 1964.

Downing, Dr. John, Article in *Reading*, UK Reading Association, Durham 1974.

Edwards, Betty, *Drawing on the Right Side of the Brain*, Los Angeles 1981 and Souvenir Press London 1981. It seems likely that the importance of this book will be increasingly recognised; it is about much more than simply drawing. Strongly recommended.

Fisher, Margery, *Intent upon Reading*, London 1961.

*Fitzwilliam Virginal Book.* A collection of Tudor music for which I cannot conveniently find a date.

Fowler, William. 'A developmental learning strategy for early reading in a laboratory nursery school,' *Interchange 2/2*. The Ontario Institute for Studies in Education, Ontario 1971.

Frankenberg, Mrs. Sidney, *Latin With Laughter*, London c.1930.

*Fuzzbuzz*, Oxford 1978. Acceptable, non-sexist reading series.

Henderson, Hazel, *The Politics of the Solar Age*, Anchor Press, Doubleday. New York 1981. 'The success of GNP measured economies rests on calling all home based and maintenance activities "non-productive".' This fine book helps us to see how we support society by standing on our own feet. It ranges very wide.

Holt, John, *Teach Your Own*, A Hopeful Path for Education, New York 1981. Many books by same author from Holt Associates; see end of Bibliography.

Hughes, J., *Phonics and the Teaching of Reading*, London 1972.
*Reading and Reading Failure*, Evans Bros., London 1975.

Hunt, J. McVicar, *Intelligence and Experience*, New York 1961.
*The Challenge of Incompetence and Poverty*, Illinois 1969.
'Social aspects of intelligence: evidence and issues.' 1971.
'Sequential Order and Plasticity in Early Psychological Development.' (Paper presented to The Jean Piaget Society, Philadelphia 1972).

Illich, Ivan, *Deschooling Society*, Calder & Boyars, London 1971. (Harper & Row, New York).

Jackson, Brian, *Your Exceptional Child*, Fontana, London 1980.

Land, Frank, *The Language of Mathematics*, John Murray, London 1960.

Leach, Penelope, *Who Cares?* Penguin, London 1979. Defends children against day-care.

Lewin, Roger (ed.), *Child Alive*, Temple Smith, London 1975.

Lister, Ian, *Deschooling*, A Reader, Cambridge University Press, 1974. A collection of articles and extracts from sources on three continents which illustrate the fact that 'more and more people are beginning to notice that majorities fail to learn what schools pretend to teach.'

Marshall, Sybil, *An Experiment in Education*, Cambridge University Press, 1963.

Montessori. *The Montessori Method*, Scientific pedagogy as applied to child education in 'The Children's Houses' with additions and revisions. With introduction by J. McVicar Hunt, Schocken Books, New York 1964.

127

Moore, Raymond S. and Moore, Dorothy N., *Better Late Than Early. A new approach to your child's education*, Reader's Digest Press, New York 1977. Two highly qualified researchers show that there is no evidence to favour early schooling, much against. Adds constructive suggestions.

Morgan, Elaine, *The Descent of Woman*, Souvenir, London 1972.

Papert, Seymour, *Mindstorms*, Children, Computers and Powerful Ideas, Basic Books, New York 1980. It appears that computers in schools are being misused as tools to teach the same old school maths. Children are capable of something better.

Péter, Rózsa, *Playing With Infinity*, Mathematics for Everyman, George Bell & Sons, London 1961. The author has the gift of showing in what way mathematics give delight.

Pines, Maya, *The Revolution in Learning*, Allen Lane, the Penguin Press, London 1971. Investigation of several different approaches to early cognitive learning in the USA. Author notes that all roads seem to lead towards early reading.

Polk-Willard, Paula, *Montessori, A Modern Approach*, Schocken Books, New York 1975. Shows Montessori to be far ahead of her time in terms of psychology of learning.

Popper, Karl, *Unended Quest*; an intellectual autobiography, Fontana, London 1976.

Porcher, Mary Ann and Winn, Marie, *The Playgroup Book*, Souvenir, New York and London 1967.

Ravielli, Antony, *Wonders of the Human Body*, Harrap, London 1955.

Richardson, Marion, *Writing and Writing Patterns*, (Twenty-seventh impression. London 1979). See 'Resources'.

Ridout, Ronald, *English Workbooks*, See 'Resources'.

Roberts, Keith, *Automation, Unemployment and the distribution of Income*, European Centre for Work & Society, 70pp, ISBN 906549 017 5, P.O. Box 3073 6202 NB, Maastricht, The Netherlands.

Thompson, H. A., *Colour-Factor Mathematics*, See 'Resources'.

Wells, J. C., *Jen Nia Mondo*, 'An introductory series of lessons in Esperanto — the living language which aims to solve the world's language problems by becoming a second language, neutral and simple, for all mankind,' Group Five, 80 Cambridge Road, Teddington, Middlesex, England, (London 1974). *Lingvistikaj Aspektoj de Esperanto*, Rotterdam 1978.

White, Burton L., *Final Report, Child Rearing Practices and the Development of Competence*, Harvard 1972.

Wyeth, Andrew, *The Two Worlds of Andrew Wyeth*, A conversation with Andrew Wyeth by Thomas Hoving. Boston 1978.


*Continuing sources of information:*

*Growing Without Schooling*, newsletter sent out six times a year from Holt Associates, 729 Boylston St., Boston, MA 02116.

*The Times Educational Supplement*, London, every week.


**References for Chapter 10**
Beacon Readers, *Teacher's Manual*, Ginn & Co. 1922-1977. Bullock, A. *A Language For Life*. H.M.S.O. 1975. Cashdan, Asher, *The Reading Teacher*, Jan. 1973. Cashdan, Asher, *Where?* July 1968. Cohen, Rachel, *L'Apprentissage Précoce de la Lecture*, 1978. Corcoran, T., Series of articles in 'Irish Monthly', June, July 1924. Diack, H., *Reading and the Psychology of Perception*, 1963. Donaldson, M., *Children's Minds*, 1978. Doman, G., *Teach Your Baby To Read*, 1965. Downing, J., *Reading* Vol. 8, No. 3. Fisher, Margery, *Intent Upon Reading*, 1961. Gibson, E., *Cognitive Development in Chldren*, Chicago, 1970. Gross, P., *Reading*, Vol. 8, No. 4. Hughes, J., *Reading and Reading Failure*, 1975. Husén, T., *The School in Question*, 1979.